eCommerce Bootcamp
Planning, Execution, Profit

Exploring the foundational areas needed before you start building your eCommerce site and a bit about website development too.

Nathan J. Neil, MBA PMP

DEDICATION

This book is dedicated to my amazing wife and sons for your steadfast love and support throughout my business ventures. You are the reason for everything that I do. This book is also dedicated to the mentors who have impacted my life; thank you for your guidance and wisdom.

Table of Contents

ACKNOWLEDGMENTS

I would like to express my deepest gratitude to all those who have contributed to the creation and completion of this book. Your support, encouragement, and guidance have been invaluable throughout this journey. I want to specifically thank all the crew members at LaunchUX, for their assistance with the development of this book.

I also want to acknowledge Kurt Wenzel, one of my earliest mentors who first introduced me to business and eCommerce when it started taking root. His life ended too soon, but during it, he had a deep and lasting impact on everyone he encountered.

CHAPTER 1
ON THE THRESHOLD OF ECOMMERCE

Over the past few decades, ecommerce has experienced remarkable growth, transforming how people buy and sell goods and services. According to Statista, global ecommerce sales have surged from approximately $1.3 trillion in 2014 to an expected $6.4 trillion by 2024. This rapid expansion has been fueled by the widespread adoption of the internet, technological advancements, and changing consumer preferences.

The rise of ecommerce has led to a decline in traditional brick-and-mortar stores. Retail giants like Sears, JCPenney, and Toys "R" Us have faced store closures and bankruptcies, highlighting the shifting landscape of retail. Many consumers now prefer the convenience and ease of online shopping, which allows them to browse and purchase products from the comfort of their homes or on the go. As a result, businesses have been forced to adapt by embracing ecommerce and finding new ways to engage with customers.

The growth of ecommerce has brought several benefits for businesses and consumers alike. Ecommerce platforms enable businesses to reach customers worldwide, eliminating geographical barriers and expanding their market. This increased access to consumers allows businesses to grow their customer base and tap into new revenue streams. Moreover, operating an ecommerce store often requires less overhead, staff, and resources than maintaining a physical storefront.

Online businesses can save on rent, utilities, and other expenses associated with brick-and-mortar locations. These savings can be passed onto consumers through lower prices or reinvested in the business to fuel growth.

Online shopping offers unparalleled convenience for customers, who can browse and purchase products anytime and from anywhere. With the ability to compare prices, read reviews, and access many products, consumers enjoy a more efficient and personalized shopping experience. Additionally, ecommerce platforms provide businesses with valuable customer data that can be used to tailor marketing campaigns and create personalized shopping experiences. This targeted approach can lead to higher conversion rates, increased customer loyalty, and more repeat business.

Ecommerce allows businesses to operate 24/7, providing customers round-the-clock access to their products and services. This flexibility enables businesses to accommodate their customers' varying needs and schedules, ultimately leading to increased sales and customer satisfaction.

The continued growth of ecommerce demonstrates its undeniable impact on the retail landscape. Businesses that recognize and capitalize on this trend have the potential to thrive in this increasingly digital world.

Challenges & Advantages to Ecommerce Business

Traditional brick-and-mortar locations have significant challenges and hurdles that can be avoided when building an online-based business. With ecommerce, you are not forced into a geographical region defined by your physical location (you can be international if you like), scaling is much easier at a smaller investment, startup costs are minimized, and you are not restricted to specific hours of conducting your business based on staffing. There are many barriers' entrepreneurs previously faced that, in the last decade or two, have been successfully eliminated. Starting a business is more accessible to anyone looking to try.

While there are significant advantages, there are challenges to be mindful of as you begin. Embarking on the journey of starting an ecommerce business can be both exciting and daunting. Entrepreneurs face numerous challenges, from choosing the right products to establishing a strong online presence. However, these challenges can be overcome with the right mindset and approach, setting the foundation for a successful ecommerce venture.

One of the key challenges new ecommerce entrepreneurs face is the vast amount of information available. Sounds like a strange remark, but it can be overwhelming to sift through all the resources, advice, and tools. To manage this information overload, it's essential to prioritize your learning and focus on the most critical aspects of your business. Break down your goals into smaller, manageable tasks and create a list of action items you can tackle individually. This will help you stay organized and maintain a sense of progress as you build your ecommerce business.

Another challenge is managing your time effectively. As an ecommerce entrepreneur, you'll likely juggle multiple responsibilities, from marketing and inventory management to customer service and order fulfillment. Developing good time management habits is crucial to stay on top of these tasks and avoiding burnout. One effective approach is the Pomodoro Technique, which involves working in focused intervals with short breaks in between. This can help you maintain productivity and prevent distractions from derailing your progress.

Setting achievable goals is essential for overcoming the challenges of starting an ecommerce business. Be realistic about what you can accomplish in each time frame and avoid setting too ambitious or vague goals. Break down your goals into smaller, specific, measurable, time-bound milestones. This will help you maintain focus and motivation as you work towards your larger objectives.

Finally, it's important to stay adaptable and be prepared to adjust your strategies as needed. The ecommerce landscape is constantly evolving, and what works today may not be effective tomorrow. Stay informed about industry trends, emerging technologies, and best practices to ensure your business remains competitive. Don't be afraid to pivot and experiment with new approaches if your current strategies aren't yielding the desired results.

By staying organized, managing your time effectively, setting achievable goals, and embracing adaptability, you'll be better equipped to navigate the challenges and set yourself on the path to success.

The Importance of Planning

Starting an ecommerce business can be demanding and complex without proper planning and research. It requires dedication, perseverance, and a positive attitude to overcome the obstacles that may arise. A well-thought-out plan will provide a solid foundation, ensuring you are prepared to tackle the various challenges and make informed decisions.

A detailed and thoughtful plan facilitates several advantages when launching your ecommerce business. First, it helps you stay organized and focused on the tasks. By outlining your goals, strategies, and timeline, you can create a roadmap that guides you through each stage of the process. This clear direction can reduce the likelihood of becoming overwhelmed by the myriad tasks of running any business and the general complexities of life.

Second, a well-crafted plan can help you allocate resources more effectively. By understanding the various aspects of your business – from inventory management to marketing and customer service – you can prioritize tasks and allocate your time, money, and energy to where they will have the most significant impact. This strategic approach can lead to more efficient operations and improved results. This is especially important when hiring contractors or employees, so they know your precise direction.

Gathering information before engaging in the development of your website is crucial for several reasons. One primary reason is that it allows you to make informed decisions about your site's design, layout, and functionality. By researching industry best practices, competitor websites, and customer preferences, you can create a website that caters to your target audience's needs and expectations. This, in turn, can result in a better user experience and higher conversion rates (increased sales).

Additionally, collecting information in advance can help you identify potential roadblocks and obstacles that may arise during the website development process. Most would be ecommerce entrepreneurs think the first thing needed is the website, but I assure you that we have much work before we get there if we are going to succeed in this endeavor. For example, understanding ahead of time the specific requirements of your payment processor (how to get paid) or shipping provider (getting the product to the buyer) can prevent delays and complications.

In the last ten years of developing ecommerce sites for clients, these crucial elements often get overlooked. All these functions need to be built into your website, but they are all relationships that must be established well before you launch. Being proactive in gathering this information can save you time, money, and frustration in the long run.

Why Not Just Sell on Amazon or Etsy

When starting an ecommerce business, entrepreneurs often decide whether to build their own website or sell their products on established marketplaces like Amazon and Etsy. Both options have their advantages and drawbacks, and it's essential to understand the differences to make an informed decision.

One of the primary benefits of owning your own ecommerce website is the control and customization it offers. This book specifically focuses on retailers looking to build and grow their brands with their own sites because, in my opinion, this is the best way to establish your brand identity, scale, and maintain control. With your own website, you have complete control over the design, layout, and overall user experience.

Having your own web presence allows you to build a unique brand identity and tailor the shopping experience to your target audience. You can also decide on specific features and functionalities that will cater to your customer's needs, helping you stand out from the competition.

Another advantage of having your own ecommerce website is the opportunity to build a direct relationship with your customers. Unlike marketplaces, where interactions are often limited, your own website allows you to communicate with customers through personalized emails, newsletters, and social media. This can help you build a loyal customer base and foster long-term relationships, leading to repeat business and positive word-of-mouth.

In terms of fees, operating your own ecommerce website can be more cost-effective in the long run. While marketplaces like Amazon and Etsy charge listing fees, transaction fees, and referral fees (usually a percentage of each sale), running your own website means you'll primarily need to cover hosting and payment processing costs associated with credit card sales. Over time, this can result in significant savings, especially as your sales volume increases.

However, there are some challenges associated with owning your own ecommerce website. One of the primary concerns is generating traffic to your site. Marketplaces like Amazon and Etsy have an existing customer base and can provide immediate exposure for your products. With your own website, you'll need to invest time and resources into marketing and search engine optimization (SEO) to attract potential customers. If you put forth the effort, you never know, a large retailer like Amazon may want to acquire you as they did in the case of Zappos.

Successful Online Retail Entrepreneurs

Numerous success stories in the world of ecommerce can serve as sources of inspiration for budding entrepreneurs.

Dollar Shave Club was founded by Michael Dubin and Mark Levine in 2011 to disrupt the traditional razor industry with its affordable and convenient subscription-based model. The company started with a viral video featuring Dubin highlighting the high cost and inconvenience of buying razors in-store. Despite initial struggles to meet the overwhelming demand, Dollar Shave Club persevered, eventually expanding its product line to include grooming and personal care items. The company's innovative approach and focus on customer experience led to its acquisition by Unilever for $1 billion in 2016.

Chewy, an online retailer of pet products, was founded in 2011 by Ryan Cohen and Michael Day. They recognized a gap in the market for a convenient and customer-focused online pet store. Starting with a small team and limited resources, Chewy focused on providing exceptional customer service, fast shipping, and a wide range of products. This dedication to customer satisfaction fueled the company's rapid growth, and in 2017, it was acquired by PetSmart for $3.35 billion.

Zappos, a well-known online shoe retailer, was founded in 1999 by Nick Swinmurn. Frustrated by the lack of selection and sizing options in traditional brick-and-mortar stores, Swinmurn saw an opportunity to create an online shoe-shopping experience with a vast selection and excellent customer service. Despite initial skepticism about the viability of selling shoes online, Zappos persevered and eventually expanded to sell clothing, accessories, and more. The company's strong emphasis on customer service and company culture attracted the attention of Amazon, which acquired Zappos for $1.2 billion in 2009.

Tattly is a temporary tattoo company founded by designer Tina Roth Eisenberg in 2011. Tired of the low-quality, uninspiring temporary tattoos available for her daughter, Eisenberg created her own line of artistically designed, non-toxic temporary tattoos. The company started small, with a handful of designs by local artists, but quickly gained traction and a celebrity following. Tattly's dedication to quality, artistic expression, and community involvement has turned it into a multimillion-dollar business.

Taylor Stitch, a San Francisco-based menswear brand, was

established in 2010 by Michael Maher, Barrett Purdum, and Mike Armenta. The trio recognized a gap in the market for high-quality, well-fitting, and sustainably produced menswear. With a focus on craftsmanship and sustainability, Taylor Stitch has built a loyal following and grown its product line to include a wide range of clothing and accessories. The company's commitment to responsible manufacturing and timeless design has set it apart in the competitive fashion world.

Viesso, a custom furniture company, was founded in 2005 by Travis Nagle and Ryan Schultz. They saw an opportunity to create an online furniture retailer that offered a unique blend of design, quality, and customization options. Starting with just a few products, Viesso grew steadily by providing excellent customer service and a seamless online shopping experience. Today, the company is a leading online retailer, offering customers a wide range of stylish and customizable furniture options worldwide.

These success stories demonstrate that a well-executed plan, perseverance, and adaptability can create a thriving ecommerce business. By learning from the experiences of these successful entrepreneurs, you can gain valuable insights and inspiration for your own ecommerce venture.

CHAPTER 2
DEVELOPING A BUSINESS PLAN

A successful ecommerce business starts with a well-crafted business plan. The importance of having a solid plan cannot be overstated, as it serves as the foundation for your entire venture. It guides your decision-making, helps you allocate resources, and provides a roadmap for achieving your goals. In this chapter, we'll discuss the key components of an ecommerce business plan, including identifying your target market, developing a value proposition, establishing a marketing strategy, creating a financial plan, and preparing for growth.

To illustrate the importance of a thorough business plan, consider two hypothetical ecommerce entrepreneurs, Alice and Bob. Alice starts her online store without a clear plan in place. She invests in inventory and marketing without fully understanding her target market, competition, or financial projections. Her lack of planning leads to poor decision-making, resulting in wasted resources and a struggling business.

On the other hand, Bob takes the time to develop a comprehensive business plan before launching his ecommerce venture. He researches his target market and competition, develops a strong value proposition, and creates a detailed marketing strategy. With a clear financial plan, Bob allocates resources effectively and monitors his business's progress. As a result, he is better prepared to face challenges, seize opportunities, and ultimately build a thriving business.

In this example, it's evident that the difference between a successful ecommerce venture and one that doesn't get off the ground can often be traced back to the presence or absence of a well-thought-out business plan. By dedicating time and effort to creating a solid plan, you can set your ecommerce business up for success from the beginning.

Identifying Your Target Market

Before you can begin selling online, you must define your ideal customer. Start by analyzing market segments and demographics to understand the characteristics of your potential buyers. Consider age, gender, location, income, and interests. For example, if you plan to sell eco-friendly clothing, your target market might include environmentally conscious consumers in the 25-40 age range with a higher-than-average income.

To better understand your target audience, you can also examine competitors in your niche and their customer base. Analyze their marketing materials, product offerings, and customer reviews to gain insights into their target demographics and preferences. This can help you identify gaps in the market or areas where you can differentiate your offering to appeal to a specific segment.

Conducting market research is another essential step in identifying your target market. You should use surveys, focus groups, or interviews to gather information about your potential customers' needs, wants, and pain points. Additionally, you can leverage online resources such as social media platforms, industry reports, and market research databases to gather valuable data about your target audience.

Creating buyer personas can be an effective way to understand your target market better. Personas are fictional representations of your ideal customers, developed based on your research and insights into your target audience. These personas help bring your target market to life by giving them names, backgrounds, and specific characteristics.

For example, "Eco-friendly Emma" might be a 30-year-old urban professional who values sustainable living and is willing to pay a premium for eco-conscious products.

Developing personas can help you visualize your target audience and make it easier to design marketing campaigns and product offerings that resonate with them. Personas can also help guide your content strategy, customer service approach, and overall brand positioning.

In addition to defining your ideal customer, it's essential to identify who is not your target market. By understanding whom you are not trying to serve, you can avoid wasting resources on marketing efforts that won't yield results. For instance, if your eco-friendly clothing line is targeted toward young professionals, you may decide not to focus on marketing to teenagers or retirees, as they may not have the same preferences or purchasing power.

It's important to remember that your target market may evolve over time as your business grows and new opportunities or challenges arise. Regularly review your target audience and personas to ensure they remain accurate and relevant. By staying in tune with your target market's preferences and needs, you can make informed decisions about your product offerings, marketing strategies, and overall business direction. This focused approach will help you build a loyal customer base and contribute to the success of your ecommerce venture.

By understanding your target audience's needs and preferences, you can tailor your products and marketing efforts to appeal to them. This focused approach will help you attract and retain customers who are most likely to be interested in your products and contribute to the growth of your ecommerce business.

Developing Your Value Proposition

To stand out in a crowded online marketplace, it's crucial to differentiate your products or services from your competitors. Your value proposition is the unique combination of features, benefits, and pricing that sets your offering apart. To craft a compelling value proposition, consider what makes your products or services special and how they address the specific needs of your target market. Communicate this unique selling proposition clearly and consistently in your marketing materials to attract and retain customers.

A value proposition clearly communicates your products or services' unique benefits to your target market. It highlights why customers should choose your brand over competitors and form the foundation of your brand identity. Crafting a compelling value proposition is critical to the success of your ecommerce business, as it helps you differentiate yourself in a crowded market and connect with your target audience on a deeper level.

There are various value propositions, each focusing on different aspects of your offering. Some businesses may emphasize product superiority, highlighting their products' unique features, design, or quality that set them apart from competitors. Others may focus on price, positioning themselves as the most affordable option in the market or offering exceptional value for money. Customer service is another potential differentiator, with businesses aiming to provide an exceptional buying experience, personalized support, or hassle-free returns.

Some examples of successful companies with strong value propositions include the following:

Apple, known for its innovative, high-quality products and seamless user experience, has built a loyal customer base by consistently delivering on its promise of cutting-edge technology and design.

Zappos, an online shoe and clothing retailer mentioned in the last chapter, differentiated itself in several ways. Their value proposition included exceptional customer service, free shipping, free returns, and a 365-day return policy to create a hassle-free shopping experience for its customers.

Warby Parker, an eyewear company, disrupted the traditional eyewear industry by offering stylish, affordable glasses through a direct-to-consumer model, eliminating middlemen, and passing the savings on to customers.

To create your value proposition, identify your unique selling points (USPs) – the aspects of your offering that set you apart from competitors. Consider your target market's needs and preferences and think about how your products or services can meet these needs in a way that no one else can.

Once you clearly understand your USPs, craft a concise, compelling statement that communicates the benefits of your offering to your target audience. This statement should be at the core of all your marketing and branding efforts, helping you connect with customers and build a strong brand identity.

Establishing Your Ecommerce Marketing Strategy

Creating a marketing plan for your ecommerce site is essential for laying the groundwork to drive traffic, increase sales, and build brand awareness. A comprehensive marketing plan should be aligned with your target audience, value proposition, and overall business goals. The following are must-haves to include and explore as you develop your marketing strategy.

Define marketing objectives: Start by outlining specific, measurable, attainable, relevant, and time-bound (SMART) goals for your future marketing efforts. These goals include increasing website traffic, improving conversion rates, growing your email list, or boosting sales within a specific timeframe. Setting clear objectives will help you focus your marketing efforts and measure your progress more effectively once your site is live.

Understand your target audience: As discussed earlier, understanding your target market is crucial for crafting effective marketing messages. Use your research and buyer personas to determine the preferences and needs of your target audience, which will guide your marketing plan.

Research marketing channels: Investigate the marketing channels that best suit your target audience, budget, and objectives. These include search engine optimization (SEO), pay-per-click (PPC) advertising, social media marketing, email marketing, content marketing, and influencer marketing. For example, if your target audience is predominantly active on Instagram, you should invest in Instagram ads and influencer partnerships.

Outline a content strategy: Develop a content plan to support your marketing objectives and engage your target audience. This can include blog posts, social media updates, email campaigns, and more. Be sure to address your target audience's pain points, interests, and needs through your content to build trust and establish your brand as an authority in your niche.

Plan website optimization: Ensure your website will be user-friendly, mobile-responsive, and optimized for search engines to increase visibility and drive traffic. Plan to implement on-page SEO best practices, such as using relevant keywords, creating engaging meta descriptions, and optimizing images to improve your site's search rankings.

Plan promotion strategies: Develop a plan for promoting your products and content across your chosen marketing channels. This may involve running targeted ad campaigns, collaborating with influencers, offering exclusive discounts, or hosting giveaways. Consider using a mix of organic and paid promotional tactics to reach a wider audience and boost brand visibility.

Measurement tools: Identify the tools and methods you'll use to track and analyze the performance of your marketing efforts once your site is live. Familiarize yourself with tools like Google Analytics to monitor website traffic, conversion rates, and other key metrics. By planning your measurement approach, you'll be ready to make data-driven decisions to optimize your marketing strategy and achieve your goals when the time comes.

Including this information and tailoring your marketing plan to encompass the above topics will help you effectively prepare to reach your target audience. Remember that your marketing plan should be considered a living document, constantly evolving, and adapting to changes in the market, customer preferences, and your business objectives.

Numerous resources are available to help individuals create effective marketing plans. These resources can range from educational articles and blog posts on marketing strategy and best practices to video tutorials and online courses offering in-depth training on specific marketing tactics.

Industry-related forums and social media groups can also provide valuable insights and networking opportunities with fellow entrepreneurs and marketing professionals. Furthermore, professional marketing consultants and agencies can offer tailored guidance and support to help you develop and implement a well-crafted marketing plan that aligns with your business goals.

Creating a Financial Plan

When developing a financial business plan for your ecommerce site, it's essential to consider various aspects of your business, including the cost of doing business, storage costs, material costs, shipping, marketing expenses, and other costs. A comprehensive financial plan should also include projections for sales, budget allocations for different areas of your business, and contingency plans for various scenarios.

To create a well-rounded financial plan, start by estimating your expenses. Begin with the cost of doing business, which encompasses aspects such as storage costs for inventory, costs of materials or goods, shipping and fulfillment fees, and any other expenses related to the operation of your ecommerce site.

These expenses can vary depending on the scale of your business and the specific strategies you choose to implement. It's important to have contingency plans for both sales surges and periods when sales may not meet expectations. Scenario planning can help you prepare for various anticipated and unanticipated situations.

When outlining your financial plan, be sure to revisit and update it regularly, comparing your projections with actual financial performance to ensure things are on track. This will help you make informed decisions and adjustments as needed.

Now that we have that established, there are some essential elements that you must include in your financial plan. Entire books are written on the topic of financial planning, but for our purposes, we are going to consider the following the most critical to plan and understand:

Sales Projections: Sales projections estimate your business's expected revenue over a specific period, such as a three-year forecast. To determine these projections, consider historical sales data, market trends, seasonality, and competitor performance. Break down your sales by product category, channel, or customer segment, and make realistic assumptions about growth rates based on your research and industry benchmarks.

Cost of Goods Sold (COGS): The cost of goods sold represents the direct costs associated with producing or acquiring the products you intend to sell. To calculate COGS, consider the costs of materials, labor, manufacturing, and any additional expenses related to obtaining the goods, such as freight or customs duties. Understanding your COGS is critical for setting appropriate prices, managing inventory, and assessing the profitability of your business.

Gross Profit Margin: The gross profit margin is calculated by subtracting the COGS from your sales projections. This figure helps you gauge the profitability of your business and informs you about your pricing strategies. A higher gross profit margin indicates a more profitable business, whereas a lower margin suggests that your business may need to cut costs or increase prices to improve profitability.

Operating Expenses: Operating expenses encompass all the costs associated with running your business that are not directly tied to producing or acquiring goods. This includes marketing, website development and maintenance, storage, shipping, salaries, professional services (consulting, photography, social media management), and other overhead expenses like rent and utilities. Categorize and list these expenses, estimating their costs over the forecast period. Keep track of industry benchmarks and best practices to ensure reasonable estimates.

Net Income Projections: Net income projections represent the potential profit your business can generate over the forecast period. To calculate net income, subtract the total operating expenses from the gross profit margin. This figure is an important measure of your business's overall financial health and can help you evaluate the viability of your ecommerce venture.

Cash Flow Projections: A cash flow projection is a financial statement that outlines the inflows and outflows of cash in your business over a specific period. This statement helps you understand when and how much cash you'll have on hand, allowing you to plan for investments, debt repayment, or potential shortfalls. Include all sources of cash inflows (e.g., sales, loans, investments) and cash outflows (e.g., operating expenses, capital expenditures, loan repayments) to create a comprehensive picture of your cash position.

Break-even Analysis: The break-even analysis determines the point at which your business covers all its expenses and begins to generate a profit. To perform this analysis, you'll need to calculate your fixed costs (e.g., rent, salaries) and variable costs (e.g., COGS, shipping) and understand how these costs change as your sales volume increases. The break-even point is reached when your total revenue equals your total costs. Knowing your break-even point can help you set sales targets and guide pricing and cost management decisions.

Capital Expenditures: Capital expenditures refer to significant investments in equipment, software, or infrastructure needed to operate your ecommerce business. These investments may include purchasing inventory management systems, warehouse equipment, or software for managing customer relationships. When outlining your capital expenditures, consider the expected useful life of these assets and their potential impact on your business's profitability and efficiency.

There are numerous resources available to help entrepreneurs with financial planning. Some of the most popular resources include the Small Business Administration (SBA), which offers a wealth of resources for entrepreneurs, such as financial planning guides, templates, and tools.

Additionally, the SBA provides access to financing options, such as loans and grants, to help entrepreneurs fund their businesses.

SCORE is another valuable resource, a nonprofit organization dedicated to helping small businesses succeed. They provide free mentoring, workshops, and webinars on various topics, including financial planning and management. Entrepreneurs can connect with experienced mentors who can provide personalized advice and guidance on financial planning.

Planning Workflows and SOPs

To run a successful ecommerce business, it's important to have a clear operational plan in place. Define your organizational structure and assign team roles to ensure smooth operations. Developing workflows and processes is essential for the smooth operation of your ecommerce business.

Creating efficient workflows and standard operating procedures (SOPs) helps ensure consistency and reduces the likelihood of errors, ultimately leading to a better customer experience.

When creating workflows, begin by mapping out each task or process within your business. This includes everything from order processing and inventory management to customer service and marketing activities. Identify the key steps involved in each process and the responsible team members or departments. Use flowcharts or diagrams to visualize the workflow, making it easier to spot bottlenecks or areas for improvement.

Once you clearly understand your business processes, you can start developing SOPs. SOPs are detailed, step-by-step instructions for carrying out specific tasks or processes. They should be clear, concise, and easy to follow, ensuring all team members can perform their duties consistently and effectively.

When writing SOPs, consider the following:

1. Define the purpose and scope of the procedure.
2. List the necessary tools, materials, or resources
3. Describe the steps required to perform the task
4. Establish quality control measures
5. Provide a method for documenting the completion of the task

Example SOP for Handling Returns

SOP	Customer Returns
Objective	To create a simple and efficient process for managing customer returns, ensuring consistency and a positive customer experience.
Scope	This SOP applies to all team members involved in processing customer returns for the ecommerce business.
Resources and Tools	Packing materials Shipping labels
Procedure	Receive return request: a. Customer submits a return request. b. Customer support sends return instructions. Customer returns the product: a. The customer returns the product, including the RMA number in the package. Inspect the returned product: a. Warehouse staff checks the returned product for damage or signs of use, ensuring it meets the conditions specified in the return policy. b. The return is approved or denied based on the product's condition. Issue Refund: a. If the return is approved, issue a refund or replacement, as per the customer's preference.

That example is watered down but does provide a good example of a framework to follow. You would want to be more detailed and outline restocking or disposal of the product. You would also want to integrate a system of documenting the process and verifying that all steps were appropriately completed.

It's important to remember that workflows and SOPs may change as your ecommerce business evolves. Be prepared to review and update these documents regularly to ensure they remain relevant and effective. Encourage feedback from team members, as they may have valuable insights into improving processes. As your business grows and adapts, your workflows and SOPs should evolve to support ongoing success.

Preparing for Growth and Scaling

When starting an ecommerce business, it's important to consider various scenarios and prepare an action plan to handle different circumstances. Planning for these situations can help you effectively manage growth, avoid pitfalls, and ensure business continuity.

Start by creating contingency plans for potential issues such as supplier disruptions, sudden changes in demand, or economic fluctuations. Identify the risks associated with each scenario and develop strategies to mitigate them. This may involve diversifying suppliers, maintaining an emergency fund, or developing backup plans for critical business operations.

Planning for growth is also essential to ensure your business can scale smoothly. Consider factors like staffing, warehouse space, and hosting resources for your website. Assess your current resources and determine the milestones you will need to expand or upgrade. For instance, you may need to hire additional staff when order volume reaches a certain threshold or move to a larger warehouse when inventory levels exceed your current storage capacity.

Establishing relationships with vendors and partners who can support your growth is important. This may include working with scalable hosting providers or partnering with third-party logistics companies to manage increased order volumes.

Investing in automation and technology can help streamline your operations and support growth. Identify areas of your business that could benefit from automation, such as inventory management or customer support. Implementing software solutions or tools can free up valuable time and resources, allowing you to focus on strategic initiatives and business expansion.

Finally, regularly review and update your plans as your business evolves. Monitor your growth, track your progress against your milestones, and adjust your plans as needed. By staying proactive and flexible, you can ensure your business is prepared to handle various circumstances and scale effectively.

Evaluating and Updating Your Business Plan

Your business plan should be a living document that evolves with you and your e-commerce venture. Regularly review your progress against your plan and adjust your strategies and goals to stay on track. Ensure that your business plan remains relevant and actionable.

In my experience, I consult my business plans quarterly to review the expectations I previously outlined and compare them against my actual performance. Sometimes I've noticed deviations or areas in which I had pivoted from my main goals. In those instances, it is important to determine if those pivots were intentional and with good justification or if you lost focus on your previous objective. I've also been known to review my business plan for expansion, such as adding products or staff. You want to ensure you do not get caught up in the moment and deviate from your plan on impulse.

There are good reasons to deviate, but you should update and restructure the plan to maintain relevance in those cases. Reevaluating and updating your business plan is crucial to staying agile and responsive to market and industry changes.

Regularly reviewing your plan allows you to identify areas where your business is excelling or falling short, allowing you to adjust your strategies and goals accordingly.

It's advisable to reevaluate your business plan at least once a year or when your industry or operations change significantly. However, conducting a more frequent review, quarterly as I do, can help you stay proactive and keep your business on track for success. When reevaluating your plan, consider the following tips:

Analyze your progress: Measure your business's performance against the goals and milestones outlined in your plan. Identify areas where you exceeded expectations or fell behind to adjust strategies and objectives accordingly.

Stay informed about market trends: Keep up to date with industry news, competitor activities, and changes in consumer behavior. This will help you identify new opportunities and potential threats, allowing you to adapt your plan to stay competitive.

Revisit your target audience and value proposition: As your business grows, your target market or value proposition may evolve. Regularly reassess these elements to ensure they align with your business's mission and objectives.

Review your financial projections: Analyze your actual financial performance against your projections. This will help you identify areas where you need to cut costs, invest more, or adjust your revenue goals.

Evaluate your operational processes: Assess the efficiency and effectiveness of your workflows and systems. Identify areas for improvement and implement changes to streamline your operations and support your business's growth.

Seek feedback from stakeholders: Gather input from your team, customers, and partners to identify areas for improvement and uncover new opportunities. This feedback can help refine your strategies and ensure your plan remains relevant and practical.

CHAPTER 3
GETTING PAID

I often observe investing in website development before addressing important foundational questions. These questions include how to get paid and how to get your product to your customers. It sounds simple, but there is much to think about and decide on. There are various types of payment processors and dozens of methods to address order fulfillment.

Selecting the right payment processor for your ecommerce site is a crucial decision that directly impacts your business's success. In this chapter, we'll explore the key factors to consider when choosing a payment processor and discuss some popular payment processing companies and their features.

When selecting a payment processor, consider factors such as transaction fees, compatibility with your ecommerce platform, ease of use, and customer support. It's essential to balance cost and functionality while ensuring that your chosen payment processor meets the needs of your business and customers. Understanding the fee structures of various processors, such as interchange plus pricing, flat percentage fees, or tiered pricing, is essential for making an informed decision.

Interchange plus pricing is a fee structure where the processor charges a fixed percentage and a per-transaction fee on top of the interchange rate. This transparent structure can be cost-effective for businesses with higher sales volumes.

Flat percentage fees are when the processor charges a single, fixed percentage for all transactions, regardless of the card type or transaction size. This simple and predictable structure may not be the most cost-effective for all businesses. Tiered pricing involves different rates based on transaction type and volume, which sometimes leads to confusion and higher costs.

Some popular payment processing companies include Authorize.net, First Data, Stripe, Square, and Intuit Payments. Each of these companies offers a range of features and benefits, so it's crucial to compare them and find the best fit for your business based on your sales volume and other specific requirements. You will need a plugin or extension to connect these payment processors to your ecommerce website. For example, WooCommerce, a popular ecommerce platform for WordPress, offers various plugins for popular payment processors. These plugins generally cost under $100 annually and allow seamless integration with your website.

Authorize.net is a well-established payment gateway that integrates with many ecommerce platforms, including WooCommerce, through a plugin. They offer a range of pricing plans, including a pay-as-you-go option, which may be attractive for smaller businesses. Authorize.net also provides advanced fraud protection tools and excellent customer support.

First Data is a global payment processing company that caters to businesses of all sizes. They offer a wide range of payment processing solutions, including mobile and point-of-sale (POS) systems. First Data provides a comprehensive suite of security features and is known for its reliability and stability. WooCommerce users can easily integrate First Data using a plugin as well.

Stripe is a popular payment processor among online businesses due to its ease of integration and developer-friendly API. Stripe supports a variety of payment methods, including credit cards, digital wallets, and local payment options. They offer a transparent pricing structure with no set-up or monthly fees, making it an attractive option for businesses of all sizes. WooCommerce offers a free Stripe plugin for seamless integration.

Square is another popular payment processor, particularly among small businesses and startups. Square offers an all-in-one payment solution that includes various tools, such as invoicing, POS systems, and ecommerce integration. They offer a simple and transparent fee structure with no monthly fee or long-term contracts.

Intuit Payments, also known as QuickBooks Payments, is an excellent choice for businesses already using QuickBooks accounting software. Intuit Payments seamlessly integrates with QuickBooks, allowing you to manage your finances and accept payments in one place. They offer competitive pricing and a range of payment processing solutions, including mobile payments, and invoicing.

It's essential to reevaluate your choice of payment processor periodically, as the best option for your business may change over time. Factors such as sales volume, business growth, and changes in the payment processing landscape can impact which payment processor is the best fit for your ecommerce site. Regularly reviewing your payment processor and comparing it to alternatives can help ensure you get the best rates and features for your business.

When choosing a payment processor, it's essential to remember the importance of security and compliance. Payment processors should adhere to the highest security standards, such as PCI-DSS compliance, to protect their customers' sensitive information. Additionally, consider the processor's track record of handling fraud prevention and its responsiveness in addressing security issues.

In summary, selecting the right payment processor for your ecommerce website is a critical decision that can significantly impact your business's success.
Take the time to research and compare different payment processing companies, considering factors such as fee structures, compatibility with your ecommerce platform, ease of use, and customer support.

Remember that your choice of payment processor should be reevaluated periodically to ensure that your business continues to get the best rates and features available. By investing time and effort in choosing the right payment processor, you can help set your ecommerce business up for long-term success.

CHAPTER 4
INVENTORY, SHIPPING, AND TAXES

One of the most critical aspects of running an ecommerce business is effectively managing inventory, shipping, and taxes (fun stuff). This chapter will delve into these topics, providing detailed information to help you navigate these essential elements of your online store.

Inventory management is crucial for any ecommerce business. Properly managing your inventory ensures you always have the right products in stock, allowing you to fulfill orders promptly and maintain customer satisfaction. A well-implemented inventory management system can also help you avoid overstocking or running out of products, which can negatively impact on your bottom line.

Start by assessing your current inventory levels, understanding the demand for your products, and identifying any patterns in sales. This information can help you create a plan for restocking, managing seasonal fluctuations, and addressing any gaps in your inventory. Consider using inventory management software or integrating your ecommerce platform with a third-party solution to streamline this process and automate tasks such as tracking stock levels and reordering products.

Both WooCommerce and Shopify offer native inventory management capabilities suitable for most businesses. These features allow you to track stock levels, set reorder points, and manage seasonal fluctuations in demand. Integrating your inventory management with your ecommerce platform also reduces the complexity of managing multiple systems and helps keep your operations streamlined and efficient.

Taxes can be a complex and often confusing aspect of running an ecommerce business. It's essential to understand the tax requirements in the countries and regions where you operate and any additional taxes that may apply to specific products or services. Be sure to research the sales tax, value-added tax (VAT), or goods and services tax (GST) rates that apply to your products and ensure that your ecommerce platform can calculate and apply these taxes correctly during the checkout process. It's also a good idea to consult with a tax professional or accountant to help you navigate the complexities of ecommerce taxation and ensure compliance with local, national, and international tax laws.

Shopify and WooCommerce both offer tax calculation features; however, as your business grows and your sales volume increases, you may need a more advanced solution. TaxJar is an excellent option for businesses that require more comprehensive tax management. It integrates easily with both WooCommerce and Shopify, automating tax calculations, filings, and reporting, making it easier to comply with tax laws in different jurisdictions.

Shipping is another crucial aspect of ecommerce operations. Providing reliable, affordable, and timely shipping options can enhance the customer experience and encourage repeat business. Start by researching various shipping carriers and their services, comparing rates, delivery times, and reliability.

Popular carriers include UPS, FedEx, USPS, and DHL. Depending on your location, you may also have access to regional to consider.

UPS is known for its reliability and extensive network, making it a popular choice for businesses shipping within the United States and internationally. They offer a wide range of services, including ground, air, and freight shipping, as well as express and time-critical options. The tracking system provided by UPS is also robust and accurate, ensuring customers can monitor their packages effectively. However, one of the disadvantages of UPS is that their services tend to be more expensive than other carriers, which can impact your profit margins.

FedEx is another popular shipping carrier with a global reach and a reputation for speedy deliveries. They offer a diverse range of shipping options, including express, overnight, and ground services and freight shipping. FedEx is known for its excellent customer service and support, making it a reliable business choice. On the downside, FedEx's pricing can also be higher than some of its competitors, and they may charge additional fees for certain services, such as Saturday delivery.

USPS is a government-operated shipping carrier in the United States and is often the most cost-effective option, particularly for small packages and shipments within the US. USPS offers various shipping services, including priority mail, first-class mail, and media mail, which cater to different needs and budgets. They also provide flat-rate shipping options, making it easier for businesses to calculate shipping costs upfront. However, the disadvantages of USPS include slower delivery times compared to private carriers like UPS and FedEx, and their tracking system may be less accurate and informative. Additionally, their services may be limited when shipping oversized or heavy packages.

DHL is a global shipping carrier with a strong presence in international markets, making it a top choice for international businesses. They offer various services, including express parcel delivery, freight transportation, and supply chain management. DHL is known for its fast and reliable international shipping services and comprehensive tracking system. One of the disadvantages of DHL is that their domestic shipping options within the United States are limited compared to carriers like UPS, FedEx, and USPS. Additionally, their pricing can be higher, especially for international shipments, which may impact your profit margins.

You could also consider using shipping platforms like ShipStation, Stamps.com, or EasyPost. These platforms consolidate shipping services from multiple carriers, allowing you to compare rates, delivery times, and reliability. This approach lets you choose the best shipping option for each order, resulting in cost savings and improved customer experience.

Once you've identified suitable shipping options, consider offering a range of choices to your customers, such as standard, expedited, and same-day shipping. Don't forget to factor in the cost of packaging materials and labor when calculating your shipping rates. Some retailers add a fee to shipping to cover this in some instances, while others consider it a cost of doing business.

From Offering Free Shipping to Using Live Rates

Amazon is known for offering free shipping on many products, especially for Prime members. To cover the shipping costs, they might slightly raise the price of the products. For instance, if the average shipping cost is $5, they could increase the product price by $5 to maintain profit margins while offering free shipping.

Another shipping strategy is employed by Gap, which offers free shipping on orders over a specific amount, such as $50. This method encourages customers to purchase more items to reach the free shipping threshold. If a customer has a cart totaling $45, they might add another item to their order to take advantage of the free shipping offer.

For several reasons, offering free shipping over a certain amount can significantly increase overall sales and encourage larger online carts. One of the primary motivators for online shoppers is the perceived value they receive from their purchases. When customers see that they can save on shipping costs by reaching a certain spending threshold, they often perceive it as a valuable deal too good to pass up.

This strategy plays on consumer psychology and the desire to maximize benefits from a transaction. When customers' cart total is close to the free shipping threshold, they are more likely to add extra items to their order to qualify for the shipping discount. For instance, if free shipping is offered for orders over $50 and a customer has a cart totaling $45, they might add another $10 item to their cart to avoid paying shipping fees. This results in a higher average order value and increases overall sales for the retailer.

Furthermore, free shipping over a certain amount can help reduce cart abandonment rates. High shipping costs are a common reason customers abandon their online carts before completing a purchase.

By offering free shipping, retailers can eliminate this barrier and increase the likelihood of customers completing their transactions.

In addition, offering free shipping over a specific amount can create a sense of urgency among shoppers. Customers who know they can only access free shipping by reaching the threshold are more likely to make impulsive purchases to take advantage of the offer. This sense of urgency can drive customers to buy more products and contribute to higher overall sales.

Selectively offering free shipping on high-margin items can be a beneficial strategy for ecommerce retailers to maintain profitability and attract customers. Retailers can absorb the shipping cost without significantly impacting their profit margins when free shipping is offered only on high-margin items. Since these items already provide a considerable profit margin, the shipping costs can be easily accommodated, allowing retailers to offer a valuable customer incentive without compromising their bottom line.

This approach can also help increase sales of high-margin products. When customers see that they can get free shipping on specific items, they may be more inclined to choose those products over others that do not have the same offer. This can lead to increased sales of high-margin items, which, in turn, contributes to overall profitability.

Moreover, offering free shipping on high-margin items can create a sense of exclusivity and value for customers. Due to the free shipping offer, they may perceive these products as more desirable or higher quality, making them more likely to purchase. This can help build brand loyalty and enhance customer satisfaction.

Offering live shipping rates is a strategy that ecommerce retailers can use to provide customers with real-time, accurate shipping costs based on factors such as destination, package weight, and package dimensions. By connecting with shipping carriers' APIs, ecommerce platforms can automatically calculate and display shipping rates to customers during checkouts. This allows customers to see the shipping cost based on the shipping method that best suits their preferences.

When offering live rates, it is essential to balance providing customers with enough options and not overwhelming them with too many choices. A good rule of thumb is to provide customers two to four shipping options. This range allows customers to make an informed decision based on their desired delivery speed and cost without causing decision paralysis.

Offering multiple shipping options can help cater to different customer preferences and expectations. For instance, some customers may prioritize fast delivery and be willing to pay a premium for expedited shipping. In contrast, others may prefer to save on shipping costs by selecting a slower, more economical shipping method. By providing a range of options, retailers can accommodate various customer needs and improve the overall shopping experience.

Moreover, offering live rates can build trust and transparency with customers. When shoppers can see the exact shipping costs and understand that they are not being overcharged are more likely to feel confident in their purchase and view the retailer as trustworthy. This can lead to higher customer satisfaction and loyalty, benefiting the retailer's bottom line.

Live rates can benefit perishable item likes those sold by Harry & David, an online gourmet food and gift retailer. These products often require expedited shipping to maintain their quality. Live rates display real-time shipping costs based on package weight, dimensions, and destination. This method allows customers to choose the most suitable shipping option for their needs and ensures that the retailer doesn't lose money on shipping costs.

For home decor items like those sold by Wayfair, flat-rate shipping might be the best option. By offering a fixed shipping fee, customers can easily determine the total cost of their purchase without any surprises at checkout. This method simplifies shipping calculations for the retailer and allows them to negotiate better rates with carriers for high-volume shipments.

Many of my clients have had much success with USPS flat-rate boxes. USPS flat-rate boxes are an excellent option for ecommerce retailers looking to simplify their shipping process and offer customers a straightforward rate. These boxes come in various sizes, and the shipping cost is determined solely by the size of the box rather than the weight or destination of the package. This allows retailers to easily determine and offer flat shipping rates for their products based on the appropriate box size.

To effectively use USPS flat rate boxes for your ecommerce business, first, analyze your product catalog and determine which products can fit into the available flat rate box sizes. Once you have identified the suitable products, group them according to the box sizes they would require for shipping. This will help you streamline your shipping process, as you can easily calculate and set flat shipping rates for each product group based on the corresponding box size.

Using USPS flat-rate boxes can offer several benefits for the retailer and the customer. For the retailer, it simplifies the shipping process and reduces the need to calculate shipping costs based on weight and destination constantly. This can save time and resources, allowing you to focus on other aspects of your business. Additionally, the predictable shipping costs make setting appropriate product pricing easier and maintaining profitability.

For the customer, flat rate shipping provides a transparent and easy-to-understand shipping cost, eliminating any unexpected fees during the checkout process. This can lead to increased customer satisfaction and a more seamless shopping experience. Furthermore, USPS flat rate boxes often include tracking and insurance, providing additional peace of mind for the retailer and the customer.

To successfully implement these shipping strategies, retailers need to calculate how much to raise product prices to absorb shipping costs for free shipping. This involves determining the average shipping cost per order by analyzing historical shipping data or obtaining quotes from multiple carriers. Once the average shipping cost is known, the retailer can incorporate this amount into the product price.

It's essential to consider market competition and ensure that increased prices don't deter customers from purchasing. Additionally, retailers should regularly evaluate shipping costs and adjust their pricing strategy as needed. It is important to maintain profitability, while offering attractive shipping options for customers.

CHAPTER 5
GETTING YOUR SITE BUILT

The foundation of your ecommerce business is your website, and several critical factors must be considered when developing it. The best starting point is selecting a good domain. A well-chosen domain name can enhance your brand's visibility and memorability. Some tips for choosing a domain name include keeping it short, easy to spell, and relevant to your business.

Consider using reputable registrars like Namecheap and Cloudflare, which provide excellent service. Domain registration generally costs around $10 to $20 per year, depending on the domain extension and registrar.

The next step in building your website is to choose the right platform. Shopify and WooCommerce are two popular choices due to their extensive features, ease of use, and availability of integrations. However, other options like Square Online, SquareSpace, BigCommerce, Wix, and Weebly are popular among those who want to do it all themselves. It's essential to research each platform to determine which one best suit your needs.

While some web builders like Square Online and Wix may be appealing due to their simplicity and user-friendly interfaces, these platforms may not be the best choice for serious ecommerce entrepreneurs. Their limited customization options and lack of advanced features can hinder your website's growth and functionality.

Shopify and WooCommerce, on the other hand, offer a wider range of integrations and support that can help your business thrive.

If you decide to build your website, numerous resources are available to help you learn the necessary skills. This chapter will briefly discuss the most popular solutions for building your own site. Later in the book in Chapter 9, I'll provide additional information specifically for DIY ecommerce entrepreneurs who want to build their own site.

Let's review a few great options for those looking to build their own site who feel comfortable with a computer but are unsure about fully building their own site.

Popular DIY Solutions and Brands Who Use Them

Wix is a user-friendly website builder that offers a wide range of templates and an intuitive drag-and-drop interface, making it easy for beginners to create a professional-looking online store. Wix's ecommerce platform includes essential features like inventory management, secure online payments, and customizable product pages. One example of an online retailer using Wix is Cuts Clothing, a premium menswear brand. The primary advantage of Wix is its ease of use, but its features and customization options may be more limited compared to more advanced platforms.

Squarespace is another user-friendly option known for its visually appealing templates and easy-to-use interface. Squarespace offers a robust ecommerce platform with features like product management, customizable product pages, and integrated payment gateways. One example of a successful online retailer using Squarespace is Kith, a famous streetwear brand. Squarespace is suitable for businesses prioritizing aesthetics, but its ecommerce features might not be as comprehensive as other platforms like BigCommerce or Shopify.

BigCommerce offers a more feature-rich ecommerce platform without the need for extensive technical expertise. It is specifically designed for ecommerce, including features like product management, payment gateways, and shipping integration. Skullcandy, a popular headphone and audio equipment brand, is one example of a successful online retailer using BigCommerce. Its comprehensive suite of ecommerce features makes it suitable for businesses of various sizes and complexity. However, BigCommerce's pricing can be higher than other platforms, particularly for businesses with significant sales volumes.

Square Online is an ecommerce platform developed by the popular payment processing company, Square. It offers a straightforward and user-friendly solution for creating an online store, with essential features like inventory management, payment processing, and customizable product pages. An example of a retailer using Square Online is Hummingbird Hammocks, a company specializing in lightweight camping hammocks. Square Online suits small businesses and those using Square's payment processing services. However, it may not be the best option for larger businesses or those with more complex ecommerce needs.

Online courses, tutorials, and forums can provide valuable guidance and support as you navigate the complexities of website development. However, it's crucial to recognize that building a professional-quality website requires a significant time investment and a learning curve is involved.

Hiring a Professional Developer

Hiring an expert web developer or agency to build your ecommerce site can offer several advantages. A professional team can bring experience, knowledge, and expertise, ensuring your website is well-designed and optimized for success. They can help with UI development, A/B testing, and ongoing support and draw upon previous projects' know-how to create a website that sets your business apart from the competition.

When selecting a web developer or agency, ask pertinent questions and carefully review their portfolio, case studies, and customer testimonials. Some questions include their experience with ecommerce websites, examples of past projects, and their approach to UI development and A/B testing. Remember that not all web development firms are created equal, so choosing a company that aligns with your business goals and vision is essential.

User Interface (UI) development is vital to any ecommerce website. A well-designed UI can significantly impact sales and user engagement. Factors such as colors, fonts, and navigation can affect the user experience, so optimizing these elements is essential. A/B testing, which involves testing different design variations to determine which performs better, can be invaluable in optimizing your website's UI. Although tools are available for conducting A/B testing, partnering with a professional web development firm can be particularly beneficial.

In website development, the key to success lies in finding a reliable and credible developer who can bring your vision to life. Separating the experts from the amateurs can be challenging with so many options available. Hopefully, the following information will prove a valuable resource for finding a trustworthy developer.

Thorough research is a crucial first step in finding a reliable website developer. Begin by searching for developers with a strong online presence, which often indicates professionalism and a commitment to their craft. A well-designed portfolio can provide insight into their skills, capabilities, and design style. A firm that showcases an extensive portfolio on its website, featuring a diverse range of projects across various industries, improves overall credibility.

In addition to examining portfolios, read client testimonials and online reviews. Don't just look at the star rating; read the reviews. These can provide valuable insight into the developer's work ethic, communication style, and ability to meet deadlines. When evaluating website developers, it's essential to consider their experience and expertise. A developer with a proven track record in creating websites similar to yours is more likely to understand your needs and deliver satisfactory results.

A strong working relationship with your developer is critical to the success of your website. Prioritize developers who prioritize communication and are willing to collaborate with you throughout the process. For example, my team at LaunchUX consistently holds meetings and updates their clients, ensuring a smooth and transparent development process.

Additionally, assess the developer's responsiveness and availability. A developer who is slow to respond or frequently unavailable might cause delays or miscommunications, potentially harming your project.

While searching for a website developer, you must know potential red flags that could signal trouble. Be cautious of developers who offer prices that seem too good to be true, as this may indicate a lack of experience or low-quality work. For example, a developer offering to build a complex website for a fraction of the industry-standard cost may not deliver the expected results.

Another red flag is a developer who guarantees specific search engine rankings or makes unrealistic promises. No developer can guarantee a particular search engine ranking, as rankings are determined by complex algorithms beyond their control. A trustworthy developer will focus on building a well-optimized website that adheres to best practices rather than making unattainable promises.

The decision to build your ecommerce website yourself or hire a professional team depends on your skills, budget, and the amount of time you're willing to invest in the project. Carefully consider your options and the resources available to make an informed decision. Remember that the right choice of platform, domain name, and UI development can significantly affect your website's functionality, performance, and ability to scale with your business's growth. Focusing on platforms like Shopify and WooCommerce can provide a solid foundation for a successful ecommerce site, while options like Wix and Weebly may be less suitable for ambitious entrepreneurs.

Web Hosting

Hosting refers to storing and maintaining your website's files on a server, which ensures that your site is accessible to visitors when they type in your web address or click on a search result. I often relate hosting to renting an office space.
Hosting is a place for your website to live and work.

Solutions like Wix, Squarespace, BigCommerce, and Square Online include hosting as part of their fees, simplifying the process of getting your ecommerce store up and running. Additionally, For Shopify, you don't need to worry about separate hosting because Shopify is a fully hosted platform, which means that hosting is already included in the monthly fees. Shopify provides a reliable and secure hosting environment, ensuring your online store runs smoothly, loads quickly, and is protected from potential security threats.

While hosting your site on platforms like Wix, Shopify, and Squarespace offers simplicity and convenience, some disadvantages exist. One of the main concerns is limited customization, as these platforms often use templates and drag-and-drop editors. For more advanced customizations, these platforms lack the flexibility to create the precise look and functionality you desire.

Another issue is that these are proprietary platforms, meaning you are tied to their ecosystem. If you decide to switch to a different platform in the future, migrating your site and its content can be challenging. You may need to rebuild your site from scratch on the new platform, which can be time-consuming and costly.

Lastly, the cost can be a drawback for some users. While these platforms offer a range of pricing plans, costs can add up over time, especially if you require additional features or apps with extra fees. Additionally, some platforms charge transaction fees instead of payment processing fees, affecting your profit margins. Where having a website built might require a larger upfront investment, these solutions tend to accumulate a larger cost overtime.

WooCommerce is a popular eCommerce platform built on WordPress, offering flexibility and customization for online stores. Unlike Wix, Shopify, and Squarespace, platforms like WooCommerce PrestaShop require you to find hosting. You must choose a hosting provider to support your eCommerce website and its requirements.

FlyWheel and WP Engine are two highly recommended hosting providers for WooCommerce, as they specialize in WordPress hosting and offer features tailored to eCommerce websites. Both hosting providers offer fast loading speeds, excellent security features, and reliable uptime, ensuring a smooth user experience for your customers. They also provide dedicated support for WooCommerce, which helps troubleshoot and optimize your online store.

When choosing a hosting provider for your eCommerce website, it's essential to consider factors such as loading speed, security, uptime, and support for your chosen platform. This ensures a stable and secure online store environment and provides customers with the best possible user experience.

If you hire a web developer, ask them about what hosting they offer. Many can offer all of this as part of a complete solution.

CHAPTER 6
DRIVING TRAFFIC & ONLINE MARKETING

Marketing your e-commerce site is essential for attracting customers, driving sales, and growing your online business. The digital landscape is highly competitive, and without a well-executed marketing strategy, your website can easily get lost in the noise. You can use various marketing techniques and channels to reach your target audience, build brand awareness, and establish trust with potential customers. This leads to increased traffic and higher conversion rates, resulting in more sales and revenue for your business.

Search Engine Optimization (SEO)

Search engine optimization (SEO) is a critical component of online marketing. It involves optimizing your website and its content to improve its visibility on search engine result pages (SERPs). By ranking higher on SERPs, your website is more likely to attract organic traffic, leading to increased sales and revenue. Key aspects of SEO include keyword research, on-page optimization, content creation, and link building. Utilize tools like Google Analytics and Google Search Console to monitor your website's performance and make data-driven decisions to improve your rankings.

SEO, is a multifaceted approach to improving a website's visibility in search engine results. It is a critical aspect of online marketing that can significantly impact a website's traffic and sales. SEO is often divided into three main categories: on-site SEO, technical SEO, and link building. Each component is essential for a comprehensive SEO strategy, and excelling in all of them is necessary to achieve the best results.

On-site SEO refers to optimizing the content and structure of a website to make it more attractive to search engines. This involves strategically incorporating relevant keywords throughout the website, creating high-quality content, optimizing title tags and meta descriptions, and ensuring a clear and logical site structure. On-site SEO helps search engines understand the topic and relevance of a website's content, which can lead to higher rankings in search results.

Technical SEO encompasses the various backend optimizations to improve a website's overall performance, accessibility, and crawlability. This includes optimizing page load speed, ensuring a mobile-friendly design, creating an XML sitemap, and implementing structured data markup. Page speed, in particular, is a crucial factor as it impacts user experience and is also considered by search engines like Google when ranking websites. A fast-loading website is more likely to rank higher in search results and attract more organic traffic.

Link building, also known as off-site SEO, involves acquiring high-quality, relevant backlinks to a website. Backlinks are hyperlinks from other websites that point to your site. They vote for confidence in your content and can significantly impact your search engine rankings. Effective link building strategies include guest posting on reputable websites, creating shareable content, and building relationships with influencers in your industry. By obtaining high-quality backlinks, you can improve your website's credibility and authority in the eyes of search engines, leading to better rankings and increased organic traffic.

Each element enhances a website's visibility in search engine results and drives organic traffic. To truly excel in the competitive world of ecommerce, businesses must pay attention to all aspects of SEO and continually refine their strategy.

Many firms may focus on one aspect of SEO and neglect others, leading to suboptimal results. For instance, a company might create excellent on-site content but overlook technical SEO, resulting in a slow-loading website that discourages users and search engines alike. On the other hand, a business may have a technically sound website but fail to acquire high-quality backlinks, limiting their site's authority and ranking potential.

To "crush it" in online sales, ecommerce businesses must invest in a well-rounded SEO strategy that addresses on-site, technical, and off-site factors. By continually monitoring and adjusting their approach, businesses can stay ahead of their competition, adapt to ever-changing search engine algorithms, and ultimately grow their online presence and sales.

Since this can be rather involved, most brands look to outsource to an SEO firm, but in doing so, make sure you are hiring one who truly knows the vast landscape of all the elements involved. It's important to consider several factors to ensure you find the right partner to achieve your goals.

First, evaluate the firm's experience and track record. Look for case studies and testimonials that demonstrate the company's success in optimizing e-commerce websites similar to yours. Choosing a firm with expertise in your industry is crucial, as they'll better understand the specific challenges and opportunities you face.

Next, examine the firm's communication style and reporting process. Effective communication is key to a successful partnership, so ensure the firm provides regular updates, reports and is responsive to your questions and concerns. This will help you stay informed about their progress and make informed decisions about your website's optimization.

Finally, discuss the firm's pricing structure and ensure it aligns with your budget. SEO services can vary significantly in cost, so it's essential to understand the scope of services you'll receive and any additional fees that may arise.

If you prefer to handle SEO in-house, several tools can provide valuable insights and help you optimize your e-commerce site effectively. Some popular options include Moz, SEMrush, and

Ahrefs. Each platform has unique advantages, and understanding their features can help you choose the right tool for your needs.

Moz is an all-in-one SEO platform that offers a range of features to help you improve your site's search engine ranking. The Moz Pro suite includes keyword research tools, rank tracking, site audits, and on-page optimization recommendations. Moz's user-friendly interface and detailed reports make it an excellent choice for beginners and experienced SEO practitioners alike. One of the standout features of Moz is its proprietary Domain Authority metric, which helps you understand the strength of your website compared to your competitors.

SEMrush is a comprehensive digital marketing platform that provides a wide range of SEO, PPC, content marketing, and social media management tools. The platform excels in competitive analysis, allowing you to benchmark your site against your competitors, uncover their organic and paid search strategies, and identify new growth opportunities. SEMrush also offers advanced keyword research tools, site audits, and backlink analysis to help you optimize your e-commerce site.

Ahrefs is another popular SEO platform known for its extensive backlink database and powerful analytical tools. Ahrefs lets you analyze your site's backlink profile, discover new link-building opportunities, and monitor your competitors' backlinks. The platform also offers keyword research tools, rank tracking, and site audits to help you optimize your on-page and off-page SEO. Ahrefs is well-suited for those looking to dive deep into backlink analysis and develop a comprehensive link-building strategy.

Numerous resources are available for individuals who want to learn more about SEO, catering to various experience levels, from beginners to advanced practitioners. Some of the best resources include blogs and websites maintained by SEO experts and companies. These sites publish valuable content about SEO strategies, news, and best practices. Popular sources include Moz Blog, Search Engine Journal, Search Engine Land, and Ahrefs Blog.

Online courses and tutorials are another excellent way to learn SEO. Many platforms offer free, paid courses that provide structured learning experiences, including video lectures, quizzes, and practical assignments. Platforms like Coursera, Udemy, and LinkedIn Learning feature a range of SEO courses that cover beginner to advanced concepts.

SEO-focused podcasts can also be a valuable resource for learning, as they often feature interviews with industry experts and discussions on the latest trends and strategies. Some popular podcasts in the SEO space include The Search Engine Journal Show, The Authority Hacker Podcast, and The SEO Podcast - Unknown Secrets of Internet Marketing.

Community forums and discussion boards, such as Reddit's r/SEO subreddit and the WebmasterWorld forum, can provide knowledge and insights from SEO professionals and enthusiasts. These platforms are great for asking questions, sharing experiences, and staying up to date with industry news and developments.

Content Marketing

Content marketing is creating and distributing valuable, relevant, consistent content to attract and engage a target audience. This approach aims to establish your business as an authority in your niche, build trust with potential customers, and ultimately drive sales.

Content marketing includes blog posts, videos, infographics, podcasts, and more. A successful content marketing strategy should focus on creating high-quality content that resonates with your target audience and addresses their needs, questions, and pain points.

A content marketing strategy is essential for attracting and retaining customers. The following example outlines a minimalistic strategy outline for GeekGear, a fictional clothing company focusing on geek and pop culture-inspired apparel.

GeekGear Content Strategy Outline

I. Define the Target Audience

GeekGear targets young adults aged 18-35 who are passionate about geek culture, including movies, TV shows, video games, and comic books.

II. Set SMART Goals

For GeekGear, SMART goals could include increasing website traffic, gaining new email subscribers, boosting social media followers, and increasing monthly sales.

III. Develop Content Pillars

GeekGear should focus on three content pillars: Geek Culture, Fashion and Style, and Behind-the-Scenes.

IV. Create a Content Calendar

A content calendar helps GeekGear plan, organize, and schedule content across various platforms.

V. Develop a Promotion Strategy

GeekGear's promotion strategy should involve social media marketing, influencer marketing, email marketing, and search engine optimization (SEO).

VI. Track and Analyze Performance Metrics

Monitor key performance indicators (KPIs) such as website traffic, social media engagement, email open and click-through rates, and conversion rates.

VII. Adjust and Optimize the Strategy

GeekGear should regularly review and adjust its content marketing strategy based on the performance metrics to ensure continued effectiveness.

Email Marketing

People often get annoyed by the volume of emails, but there is a reason they get sent. Email marketing is a powerful tool for building customer relationships and driving sales. By building a targeted email list and sending out regular newsletters and promotional materials, you can inform your subscribers about new products, sales, and other updates.

Email marketing also enables you to segment your audience and tailor your messaging to suit different customer groups. This personalization can lead to higher open and click-through rates, ultimately driving in more sales.

Several email marketing platforms can help you manage and optimize your email campaigns, such as Mailchimp, Constant Contact, Sendinblue, and GetResponse. These platforms offer features like customizable email templates, list segmentation, analytics, and automation, making creating and managing email marketing campaigns easy.

When building a strong email database, focusing on quality over quantity is essential. A well-targeted email list can drive better engagement and conversions than a larger but less relevant list. Here are some tips for building a good email database.

Offer value to your subscribers: Encourage visitors to sign up for your email list by providing exclusive content, discounts, or access to special promotions. Make it clear what benefits they'll receive by subscribing.

Use multiple sign-up opportunities: Place email subscription forms strategically throughout your website, such as in the header, footer, or as a pop-up. You can also include a sign-up option to capture customers' email addresses during checkout.

Create compelling opt-in forms: Make your opt-in forms visually appealing and easy to fill out. Keep the form fields minimal, usually just an email address and possibly a name, to reduce friction and increase the sign-up likelihood.

Be transparent about privacy: Assure your potential subscribers that their information will be kept confidential and used only for their agreed purposes. Clearly state your privacy policy and include a link on your sign-up forms.

Segment your email list: As your email database grows, segment your subscribers based on purchase history, browsing behavior, or demographics. This will allow you to send targeted, relevant content that resonates with your subscribers and drives higher engagement.

Monitor and clean your list regularly: Keep track of your email list's performance and engagement metrics. Remove inactive subscribers and maintain a healthy, engaged list to improve your email deliverability and campaign results.

By combining the right email marketing platform with a well-maintained email database, you can effectively engage with your customers and drive sales for your e-commerce site. When determining the success of an email marketing campaign, it's essential to evaluate several key metrics:

1.   **Open rate:** This measures the percentage of recipients who opened the email. A higher open rate indicates that your subject lines effectively capture your subscribers' attention.

2.   **Click-through rate (CTR):** This measures the percentage of recipients who clicked on a link within the email. A higher CTR indicates that your content is engaging and relevant to your audience.

3.   **Conversion rate:** This is the percentage of recipients who clicked on a link within the email and completed a desired action, such as purchasing or signing up for an event. A high conversion rate suggests your email campaign drives results and meets your business objectives.

4. **Bounce rate:** This measures the percentage of emails not delivered to recipients for various reasons, such as invalid email addresses or full mailboxes. A lower bounce rate is desirable as your emails reach your intended audience.

5. **Unsubscribe rate:** This is the percentage of recipients who opt out of your email list after receiving an email. A high unsubscribe rate may indicate that your content is not resonating with your audience or that you are sending emails too frequently.

6. **Revenue generated:** Calculate the total revenue generated from the email campaign by tracking sales attributed to the campaign. This will help determine your email marketing efforts' return on investment (ROI).

Social Media Marketing

Social media marketing is essential for ecommerce businesses, as it allows you to connect with your audience, create brand awareness, and drive traffic to your website. To make the most of your social media marketing, share engaging content relevant to your target audience and encourage interaction.

This can include product promotions, behind-the-scenes looks, customer stories, or educational content. Use a mix of content types, such as images, videos, and articles, to keep your audience engaged.

User-generated content is another effective strategy. Encourage your customers to create content featuring your products and share it on their social media profiles. This can help build trust and credibility while increasing your brand visibility.

Consider collaborating with influencers who have a significant following in your niche. They can help promote your products and increase brand exposure by creating sponsored content or participating in giveaways.

Running targeted ads on platforms like Facebook or Instagram is a great way to reach your target audience. Implement pixel tracking to track conversions and optimize your ad campaigns based on data.

When determining which social networks to invest time in, it's essential to understand each platform's demographics and user behaviors. With over 2.8 billion monthly active users, Facebook's diverse user base spans various age groups, locations, and interests. It's an excellent platform for reaching a wide audience and running targeted ad campaigns.

Instagram, popular among younger audiences, especially those aged 18-34, focuses on visual content, such as images and videos. It's ideal for businesses with visually appealing products or creative content.

Twitter's user base leans towards a younger, more educated demographic. The platform is suitable for sharing timely updates, engaging in conversations, and connecting with industry influencers. By considering each platform's demographics and user behaviors, you can effectively allocate your time and resources to your business's most relevant social networks.

Pay-Per-Click Advertising (PPC)

Pay-per-click (PPC) advertising, such as Google Ads and Bing Ads, offers a wide range of targeting options to reach your desired audience. By carefully selecting your targeting criteria, you can ensure your ads are shown to the most relevant users, increasing the likelihood of conversions.

Some common targeting criteria include age, location, interests, search phrases, and demographics. Age targeting allows you to show your ads to users within specific age groups, ensuring your products or services are presented to an audience most likely to be interested. Location targeting enables you to focus on users within specific geographic areas, which can be especially helpful for local businesses or those with a regional focus. Interest targeting helps you reach users based on their interests, browsing behavior, or the types of websites they visit.

Keyword targeting is crucial in PPC advertising, as it allows your ads to be displayed when users search for specific phrases related to your products or services. Carefully selecting and optimizing your keywords ensures your ads are shown to users with a high intent to purchase.

Demographic targeting lets you focus on users with demographics, such as gender, education level, or household income, ensuring your ads are shown to the most relevant audience.

Google AdWords, the most popular PPC platform, offers robust targeting options and a vast user base due to its dominant market share. Google provides detailed data and analytics, allowing advertisers to optimize their campaigns and maximize their return on investment. However, Google Ads can be competitive and, in some cases, expensive due to the high demand for popular keywords.

While less popular than Google AdWords, Bing Ads still provides a valuable advertising platform. Although it has a smaller user base, Bing Ads can offer lower costs per click and less competition for keywords. This can be advantageous for smaller businesses or those with limited advertising budgets.

Other alternatives include social media advertising platforms such as Facebook Ads, Instagram Ads, or LinkedIn Ads, which offer unique targeting options and user demographics.

Influencer Marketing

Influencer marketing has emerged as a powerful promotional tool in recent years. It involves partnering with influential individuals, often on social media platforms, who can promote your products or services to their followers. By leveraging the trust and credibility that influencers have built with their audience, you can effectively reach potential customers and boost your brand awareness.

Several types of influencer marketing include sponsored posts and product reviews, collaborations, and event appearances. Some products and services that work well with influencer marketing include fashion, beauty, health and wellness, travel, and technology.

However, almost any niche can benefit from influencer marketing if the right influencer is chosen.

To identify potential influencers to partner with, you should first determine your target audience and the social media platforms they frequent. Next, look for influencers with a strong following on those platforms whose content aligns with your brand and target audience.

Remember that the size of the influencer following is not always the most crucial factor. Sometimes, smaller influencers, or "micro-influencers," can have a highly engaged audience and may provide better results.

When evaluating potential influencers, consider their engagement rates, which include likes, comments, and shares. High engagement rates indicate that their audience is interested in and responsive to their content. Additionally, assess the authenticity and credibility of their content, as this will impact how their followers perceive your brand.

Once you have identified potential influencers, submit a proposal outlining your partnership goals, the type of content you'd like them to create, and the compensation you offer. Compensation can take various forms, such as monetary payments, free products or services, or cross-promotion opportunities.

Choosing the right influencers for your target demographic is crucial for the success of an influencer marketing campaign. The right influencer can help a brand connect with its audience and build trust, while a poor choice can hurt the brand's reputation and even backfire.

An example is Swedish YouTuber PewDiePie, whom Disney and YouTube dropped after he posted videos containing anti-Semitic content. Brands partnered with PewDiePie faced backlash for associating with the controversial content creator, leading to severed business relationships and reputational damage.

Conversion Rate Optimization (CRO)

With the broad array of options to drive traffic to your site, you will want to determine the most effective and generate the most revenue. Conversion Rate Optimization (CRO) is the process of improving the effectiveness of your website and marketing efforts to increase the percentage of visitors who take the desired action, such as making a purchase or signing up for a newsletter. Measuring CRO is vital for new businesses to understand how well your website and marketing channels perform and make data-driven decisions to enhance your strategies.

To measure CRO, you need to track and analyze various metrics, such as website traffic, conversion rates, bounce rates, average time on page, and other user behavior data. Web analytics tools like Google Analytics can help collect and analyze this information. By setting up conversion goals and tracking events, you can measure the effectiveness of your website and various marketing channels in driving conversions.

Attributing conversions to specific marketing channels can be achieved through attribution models. Attribution models assign credit for conversions to different touchpoints in a user's journey, helping you understand which channels contribute most to your conversions. Google Analytics offers several predefined attribution models, such as the Last Interaction, First Interaction, and Linear models. You can also create custom models based on your unique business needs and objectives.

For instance, the Last Interaction model assigns full credit to the final touchpoint before the conversion. In contrast, the First Interaction model attributes the conversion to the first touchpoint in the user's journey. The Linear model, on the other hand, distributes credit equally among all touchpoints. By analyzing the performance of your marketing channels through different attribution models, you can gain insights into which channels are most effective in driving conversions and allocate your marketing resources accordingly.

CHAPTER 7
ESSENTIAL POLICIES AND SECURITY

Ensuring the security of an ecommerce website is critical for protecting customers' personal and payment information. This chapter will explore various aspects of ecommerce security, including creating a returns policy, crafting a privacy policy, maintaining security updates, testing website vulnerabilities, and developing a plan to address potential security breaches.

Security and transparency are particularly crucial for small online retailers, as they often face the challenge of establishing their credibility and reliability in the eyes of consumers. Unlike well-known brands that have already earned the trust of their customers, small businesses must work diligently to demonstrate their commitment to protecting sensitive information and providing a secure shopping experience.

Returns & Privacy Policy

A returns policy is an essential component of an ecommerce business that outlines the terms and conditions under which customers can return, or exchange purchased items. This policy not only offers protection for the seller by establishing clear guidelines for returns, but it also benefits the consumer by providing them a sense of security when shopping online. By having a transparent and fair returns policy, businesses can demonstrate their commitment to customer satisfaction, fostering trust and encouraging repeat business.

A well-crafted returns policy should include information on the timeline for returns, the condition of the product required for a return, refund options, return shipping procedures and any exceptions to the policy. It is crucial to communicate this information clearly to avoid misunderstandings and potential customer disputes. A comprehensive returns policy for the seller can help streamline the return process, reduce fraudulent returns, and improve customer relations.

A well-known example of a poorly written return policy is the case of Forever 21. In 2017, the company faced backlash from customers after it was revealed that their return policy had been changed without notice. The new policy stated that items could only be exchanged or returned for store credit within 21 days of purchase and that all sales were final on discounted items.

This new policy confused customers, as many were unaware of the changes and were left with items they couldn't return or exchange. As a result, customers took to social media to express their frustration, and many vowed to stop shopping at Forever 21.

The negative publicity caused by the poorly written return policy significantly impacted on the company's reputation and bottom line. Forever 21 was forced to revise its policy and issue a public apology to customers to regain their trust and maintain its brand image.

This example underscores the importance of having a clear and concise return policy that is communicated effectively to customers. A poorly written policy can result in confusion and frustration among customers, leading to negative publicity and a loss of business. Look at the following example for a minimalistic return policy to get started.

Return Policy Example

At [Your Business Name], customer satisfaction is our top priority. If you are not completely satisfied with your purchase, you may return the item(s) within 30 days of the delivery date for a refund or exchange.

Please note the following conditions for returns:

1.   Items must be in their original condition, unused, unworn, and with all tags and packaging intact.
2.   Return shipping costs are the customer unless the item is faulty or incorrect due to an error on our part.
3.   Refunds will be issued to the original payment method within 5-7 business days of receiving the returned item(s).
4.   Exchanges are subject to availability. If the desired replacement item is not in stock, a refund will be issued instead.

All sale and discounted items are considered final and cannot be returned or exchanged.

To initiate a return, please contact our customer service team at [email address] or [phone number] with your order number and a brief description of the issue.

Our team will provide you with further instructions on how to proceed with your return.

A privacy policy, however, is a legal document that outlines how an ecommerce business collects, uses, and protects customers' personal information. This policy is critical for building customer trust and demonstrating compliance with data protection laws, such as the General Data Protection Regulation (GDPR). A privacy policy should cover the types of personal information collected, how it is used and protected, how customers can access and control their information, and compliance with relevant data protection laws.

If you use tools like Google Analytics, Facebook Pixel, and similar tracking technologies, it is essential to disclose this information in your privacy policy. These tools collect data on user behavior and preferences, potentially considered personal information. Disclosing the use of these tools helps maintain transparency and ensures compliance with data protection laws, such as GDPR and the California Consumer Privacy Act (CCPA).

To disclose the use of these tools in your privacy policy, you should include a section dedicated to explaining the tracking technologies you employ on your website. You should mention the specific tools you use, such as Google Analytics and Facebook Pixel, and briefly explain their purpose.

For instance, you can explain that Google Analytics helps you understand how users interact with your website, allowing you to improve user experience. Facebook Pixel helps you optimize your advertising campaigns by tracking user actions on your site.

You should also explain the type of data these tools collect and how this data is used. For example, Google Analytics collects information about the pages visited, the amount of time spent on each page, and the user's location, among other data. Similarly, you can mention that Facebook Pixel collects data on user behavior, such as clicking on ads or completing a purchase, which helps you create targeted advertising campaigns.

Lastly, it is crucial to provide information on how users can opt out or manage their preferences regarding these tracking technologies. You can include links to the respective privacy policies of Google Analytics, Facebook Pixel, and other tools you use, which typically contain information on how users can control their data collection settings. Additionally, you can mention any cookie consent management tools or browser settings users can utilize to manage their tracking preferences.

By clearly disclosing tracking technologies like Google Analytics and Facebook Pixel in your privacy policy, you maintain transparency with your users and ensure compliance with relevant data protection laws, fostering trust and promoting a secure online shopping environment.

Several online resources can help new businesses create a privacy policy. For instance, there are templates and guides available that offer a starting point for drafting these policies.

Additionally, tools such as the Privacy Policy Generator can assist in creating a policy that is accurate and compliant with relevant laws. It is also advisable to consult with a legal expert to ensure that the policies are up-to-date and adhere to the specific requirements of the business's jurisdiction.

Maintaining Security Updates

The importance of keeping your e-commerce system, plugins, and themes up to date cannot be overstated. Regular updates help ensure your website remains secure and functional, protecting your business and customers' sensitive information. In one incident, I personally observed that a slider plugin that placed graphics across the top of an e-commerce website had a vulnerability that the plugin developer found and fixed. The company that ran the site never installed the update and, in the end, experienced a security breach. This breach led to the theft of customers' personal and payment information, causing significant damage to the company's reputation and customer trust.

Updating your e-commerce system's themes is equally essential, as outdated themes may contain security vulnerabilities or compatibility issues with newer versions of plugins and e-commerce platforms. These issues can result in a poorly functioning website, negatively impacting the user experience and potentially exposing sensitive data.

When working with a web development agency, it's crucial to inquire about their ongoing update support services. Some agencies may not automatically renew plugin subscriptions or inform you when additional licensing is required, leaving your website vulnerable to security risks. To ensure your website remains up-to-date and secure, it's essential to establish a clear understanding of the agency's responsibilities in terms of updates, subscriptions, and licensing.

Testing Website Vulnerabilities

Regularly testing website vulnerabilities is crucial in maintaining ecommerce security. Several tools are available to help identify potential weaknesses on a website, including free and paid options.

One popular tool is OWASP ZAP (Zed Attack Proxy), a free, open-source tool designed to test web application security. It features a user-friendly interface, including automated scanners, intercepting proxies, and passive scanners. ZAP identifies vulnerabilities like SQL injection, cross-site scripting (XSS), and authentication issues.

Another free option is the Vega scanner, which is open-source and designed to test web application security. Vega includes automated scanners, proxy interception, and a comprehensive reporting system. Vega is known for being easy to use and is a popular choice for those new to website security testing.

Burp Suite is a popular choice for those looking for a paid option. Burp Suite includes a comprehensive set of tools designed to test website security, including manual and automated scanning options. It includes active and passive scanning features, a proxy intercepting tool, and an intruder tool for testing authentication. Security professionals widely use Burp Suite, which offers a free trial before committing to a paid plan.

Another paid option that is worth considering is the Securi Site Scan. Securi Site Scan offers free and paid options for website scanning, including a range of features such as malware detection, blacklist monitoring, and firewall protection. The tool is known for its user-friendly interface and can effectively identify and prevent website security vulnerabilities.

As mentioned earlier, it's important to remember that regular updates to a website's operating system, web server software, and plugins are critical in maintaining security.

Developing a Plan to Address Potential Security Breaches

Even with these security measures in place, there is still a risk of a security breach. This is why it's crucial to have a plan to address potential security breaches and risks. This plan should include steps for minimizing the impact of a breach, such as notifying customers of the breach and taking steps to prevent future breaches.

A security breach can cause significant damage to a business's reputation and result in legal and financial consequences. By having a plan in place, ecommerce business owners can minimize the impact of a breach and demonstrate their commitment to protecting their customers' personal and payment information.

When developing a breach plan, it's important to consider a range of scenarios, including data breaches, website hacking, and employee theft. A breach plan should include the following steps:

Identify the breach: As soon as a breach is suspected, it's essential to identify the source and extent of the breach. This may involve conducting a forensic analysis of the affected system or device to determine how the breach occurred.

Contain the breach: Once the source and extent have been identified, it's vital to contain the breach to prevent further damage. This may involve isolating affected systems, shutting down compromised accounts, or disabling access to sensitive information.

Notify affected parties: If customer data has been compromised, it's crucial to notify them immediately. This may involve sending email notifications or issuing public statements to inform customers of the breach and provide information on steps they can take to protect their personal information.

Investigate the breach: After the breach has been contained and affected parties have been notified, thoroughly investigate the breach. This may involve hiring a third-party forensic expert to review the affected systems comprehensively.

Improve security measures: Based on the investigation findings, improving security measures is important to prevent future breaches. This may involve implementing additional security protocols, updating software and systems, or providing additional employee training.

Implementing strong security measures is crucial in preventing data breaches. The Equifax breach in 2017 resulted in the theft of personal information, including Social Security numbers and credit card numbers, of 143 million people. The Target breach in 2013 resulted in the theft of credit and debit card information from 40 million customers.

Both breaches could have been prevented by implementing more robust security measures, such as two-factor authentication and additional encryption. In addition to HTTPS, SSL certificates, and tokenization, other security practices include using strong passwords and two-factor authentication.

Examples of companies that have responded effectively to breaches include Target and Equifax. Target responded to a data breach in 2013 by quickly notifying affected parties, offering free credit monitoring to affected customers, and implementing additional security measures to prevent future breaches.

Similarly, Equifax responded to a data breach in 2017 by offering free credit monitoring and identity theft protection to affected customers and implementing additional security measures to prevent future breaches.

CHAPTER 8
ADAPTABILITY & MINDSET

In the ever-evolving world of ecommerce, persistence and adaptability are essential for success. As technology advances and consumer preferences change, online retailers must stay agile and open to new opportunities to stay ahead of the competition.

The ecommerce landscape is constantly shifting, and businesses must be able to adapt to these changes to stay relevant and maintain growth. Amazon is a prime example of a company successfully adapting to market changes. What began as an online bookstore has now become the world's largest ecommerce platform, offering a wide range of products and services. This transformation was made possible by Amazon's ability to recognize and capitalize on new opportunities and its persistent pursuit of innovation.

Another example is the fashion brand Zara, which has succeeded in quickly adapting to changing fashion trends. By utilizing a fast-fashion model and a highly responsive supply chain, Zara can produce and distribute new styles in weeks, allowing it to stay ahead of competitors and meet ever-changing consumer demands.

Identifying new opportunities and trends

To adapt to market changes and identify new opportunities, ecommerce businesses must stay informed about industry trends and consumer behavior. By monitoring the market and analyzing customer data, businesses can identify emerging trends and adjust their product offerings accordingly. Tools such as Google Trends, market research reports, and social listening can help businesses stay up to date with the latest developments in their industry.

For example, the rise in popularity of eco-friendly products has led many ecommerce businesses to incorporate sustainable practices into their operations and offer environmentally friendly products. By staying attuned to this trend, these businesses have been able to capitalize on the growing consumer demand for sustainable goods.

Learning from the flops

In the world of e-commerce, success stories abound, but equally important are the lessons we can learn from the failures of others. Some well-known failed online businesses offer valuable insights into the pitfalls and challenges that e-commerce entrepreneurs may face.

Kozmo, an online delivery service founded in 1998, aimed to revolutionize the delivery industry by providing one-hour delivery for various products, including DVDs, snacks, and other small items. However, Kozmo's business model proved unsustainable due to its high operating costs, lack of a clear revenue strategy, and reliance on a small delivery fleet. The company reportedly burned through nearly $280 million in funding before shutting down in 2001. A more efficient delivery model, such as partnering with existing delivery services, or focusing on specific niche markets, might have prevented Kozmo's collapse.

Boo.com, an ambitious fashion retailer launched in 1999, received over $135 million in funding and had high expectations due to its impressive marketing budget and high-profile founders. However, their complex and slow-loading website design and a lack of focus on customer experience alienated users and led to dwindling sales. When the company went bankrupt in 2000, it had lost nearly all of its invested capital. A more user-friendly website and better customer service might have saved Boo.com from failure.

Pets.com, which aimed to become the go-to online destination for pet supplies, launched in 1998 with high hopes. Despite raising more than $82 million in funding and achieving significant brand recognition, Pets.com faced intense competition from other online retailers and struggled with high shipping costs for their bulky products. When the company folded in 2000, it had lost millions of dollars. To survive, Pets.com might have needed to find a unique selling proposition or target a specific niche within the pet market.

eToys, an online toy retailer founded in 1997, attracted more than $166 million in funding and expanded rapidly, but it failed to compete with industry giants like Amazon and Toys "R" Us. Issues such as poor inventory management and an aggressive, unsustainable expansion plan led to eToys' bankruptcy in 2001. Better supply chain management and a more strategic approach to growth could have helped eToys stay afloat.

Webvan, an online grocery delivery service launched in 1999, aimed to disrupt the grocery industry but faltered due to high infrastructure costs and an overly ambitious expansion plan. Despite raising over $800 million in funding, Webvan declared bankruptcy in 2001. A more gradual and targeted growth strategy and cost control measures could have made a difference for Webvan.

Fab.com, a design-focused e-commerce company founded in 2010, initially experienced rapid growth and attracted over $330 million in funding. However, it ultimately failed due to rapid expansion, excessive spending, and an inability to maintain a unique value proposition. Fab.com laid off 80% of its staff and eventually sold its assets to PCH International for a fraction of its peak valuation. A more focused approach and disciplined financial management could have saved Fab.com.

Jux, a content-sharing platform that aimed to compete with giants like WordPress and Tumblr, failed to differentiate itself from the competition and eventually shut down in 2012. Jux might have found success by carving out a unique niche or developing a more innovative feature set. Quirky, a platform for inventors to submit ideas and have them developed into consumer products, raised more than $180 million in funding but struggled with an unsustainable business model and high manufacturing costs. A more efficient manufacturing process and better financial management could have saved the company.

Finally, Rdio , a music streaming service founded in 2010, was one of the early players in the market but eventually lost out to competitors like Spotify and Apple Music. Despite raising more than $117 million in funding, Rdio struggled to attract a large user base and differentiate itself from its competitors. The company filed for bankruptcy in 2015, and Pandora acquired its assets. A more aggressive marketing strategy and a focus on creating unique features or exclusive content could have helped Rdio survive in the competitive music streaming landscape.

Secret, an anonymous social network launched in 2014, raised over $35 million in funding but faced significant backlash due to cyberbullying and privacy concerns. Despite a promising start, Secret's user base quickly dwindled, and the company shut down in 2015. A stronger focus on user safety and privacy and better moderation tools might have saved Secret from its demise.

These ten examples of failed e-commerce ventures highlight the importance of learning from others' mistakes. Key takeaways include the need for a sustainable business model, efficient cost management, a unique value proposition, strategic growth, and a focus on customer experience. By studying these failures, e-commerce entrepreneurs can gain valuable insights and avoid similar pitfalls in their own ventures.

Tips from entrepreneurs and stories of success

Staying focused and building a strong brand is essential to success in the ecommerce space. Several well-known entrepreneurs have shared their insights on maintaining focus and growing a brand.

Jeff Bezos, the founder of Amazon, has emphasized the importance of focusing on customer needs and constantly innovating to meet those needs. He has said, "If you're competitor-focused, you have to wait until a competitor is doing something. Being customer-focused allows you to be more pioneering."

When Amazon was started in 1994 by Jeff Bezos, it was a small online bookstore that operated out of Bezos' garage in Seattle. Bezos had a vision for an online store that could offer a wider selection of books than traditional bookstores and deliver them directly to customers' homes. Despite facing skepticism from investors and critics who doubted the viability of online retail, Bezos persevered and eventually expanded the company's offerings to include a wide range of products and services.

Today, Amazon has become a behemoth of the tech industry, with a market capitalization of over $1.5 trillion as of 2021. The company's offerings have expanded beyond retail to include cloud computing, digital streaming, and even brick-and-mortar stores. Amazon is now the largest online retailer in the world, with a dominant market share in many countries. The company's logistics and supply chain management innovations have revolutionized the retail industry, and its influence is felt across a wide range of sectors. Despite criticism for its labor practices and impact on small businesses, Amazon remains one of the world's most successful and influential companies.

Steve Jobs, a co-founder of Apple, stressed the importance of prioritizing and simplifying, saying, "That's been one of my mantras — focus and simplicity. Simple can be harder than complex; you have to work hard to get your thinking clean to make it simple."

Death Wish Coffee is a great example of an ecommerce business that has succeeded by keeping things simple. The company's focus on selling high-quality coffee beans and related products has resonated with customers who are looking for a straightforward and reliable source of caffeine.

One way that Death Wish Coffee keeps things simple is by focusing on just a few core products. The company's flagship product is its

Death Wish Coffee blend, which is billed as the "world's strongest coffee." In addition to the coffee beans themselves, the company also sells related products like coffee mugs and accessories. By focusing on a few key products, Death Wish Coffee is able to maintain a high level of quality and consistency across its offerings.

Another way that Death Wish Coffee keeps things simple is by offering a straightforward and easy-to-use ecommerce platform. Customers can easily browse the company's products, place orders, and track shipments through the company's website. The website is designed to be user-friendly and intuitive, with a focus on providing a streamlined shopping experience.

Death Wish Coffee also keeps things simple when it comes to marketing and branding. The company's branding is centered around its "Death Wish" theme, with bold, edgy graphics and messaging that appeal to coffee lovers looking for a strong and powerful brew. The company's marketing efforts are focused on building a loyal following of customers through social media and other online channels.

Richard Branson, the founder of the Virgin Group, has spoken about the importance of taking calculated risks and not being afraid to pivot when necessary, saying, "You don't learn to walk by following rules. You learn by doing and falling over."

Dollar Shave Club is one example of a risky ecommerce business that became successful. The company was founded in 2011 with the goal of disrupting the shaving industry by offering a subscription-based model for delivering razors and other grooming products directly to customers' doors.

At the time, the shaving industry was dominated by a few major players who controlled most of the market share. Dollar Shave Club's decision to enter this crowded market with a subscription-based business model was seen as a risky move by many industry experts.

However, Dollar Shave Club was able to succeed by differentiating itself from its competitors through its marketing and branding. The company's marketing campaigns, which featured humorous and irreverent videos that went viral on social media, helped to establish a strong brand identity and build a loyal following of customers.

Dollar Shave Club also kept costs low by focusing on a few core products and using a direct-to-consumer model to cut out the middleman. This allowed the company to offer competitive pricing on its products and maintain a high level of customer satisfaction.

The company's success caught the attention of Unilever, one of the world's largest consumer goods companies, which acquired Dollar Shave Club for $1 billion in 2016. The acquisition was a testament to the success of Dollar Shave Club's risky ecommerce business model and its ability to disrupt an established industry through innovative marketing and branding.

One last success story that hits on a significant area of consideration as you start your journey that I haven't discussed much developing a community around your product. For Eric Banholz a simple blog turned into a very successful venture. Eric Banholz decided to grow a beard and turned an online community into an ecommerce business that generates $20,000 a day. Eric was frustrated with the lack of grooming products available for bearded men, which sparked his journey. Beardbrand is a company that has made a name for itself by producing high-quality grooming products for men.

At first, Beardbrand was just a blog where Bandholz would share his experiences and tips on growing and maintaining a beard. However, as the blog grew in popularity, Bandholz realized that there was a market for high-quality grooming products for bearded men.

The company's initial focus was on producing beard oils made with natural ingredients and designed to keep beards healthy and well-groomed. The oils quickly became popular, and Beardbrand began to expand into other grooming products like beard balms, mustache waxes, and combs.

One of the key factors that helped Beardbrand grow into a successful ecommerce store was its focus on building a community around its products. The company recognized that there was a growing trend of men growing and maintaining beards, and it saw an opportunity to connect with this community and offer products that met their needs.

To build this community, Beardbrand focused on creating high-quality content that appealed to men interested in grooming and style. This included blog posts, videos, and social media content that provided tips and advice on how to grow and maintain a beard and advice.

Beardbrand also focused on creating a seamless customer experience, with a website that was easy to use and navigate, and fast and reliable shipping. The company also offered a money-back guarantee on all its products, which helped build customer trust and confidence.

We've hit on a lot of these topics in this book and by focusing on creating high-quality content and engaging with their target audience, Beardbrand was able to build a loyal following of customers who were passionate about their products. Another important lesson we can take from this is the importance of branding and creating a strong brand identity that resonates with your target audience. Beardbrand's branding was designed to appeal to men interested in grooming and style, and the company's products and packaging reflected this.

Finally, Beardbrand's focus on creating a seamless customer experience and offering a very simple return policy. By prioritizing customer satisfaction, Beardbrand was able to build a reputation for quality and reliability that helped drive sales and grow its ecommerce store.

With these tips, ecommerce entrepreneurs can stay focused on their goals, build a strong brand, and adapt to the ever-changing market landscape.

Looking at the road ahead

Starting and running an ecommerce business can be an exciting yet challenging journey. Staying focused, tracking your progress, and maintaining a positive mindset even when faced with setbacks are essential. Let's explore tips on measuring your successes, navigating the inevitable challenges, and maintaining a positive outlook during your ecommerce journey.

Don't forget to celebrate your successes, no matter how small. Recognizing your accomplishments and progress can help keep you motivated and maintain a positive outlook. There are various good ways to celebrate business successes, such as acknowledging and recognizing individual contributions if you have employees. Publicly acknowledging the efforts of team members and highlighting their contributions can boost morale and motivate others to work towards similar achievements.

Hosting a company-wide event, such as a party or team building activity, is another great way to celebrate business successes. This can be a fun and relaxed way to bring everyone together to recognize the hard work that went into achieving the success. Incentives or rewards, such as bonuses or promotions, can also be offered to celebrate business successes and provide motivation for employees to continue working towards future successes.

Additionally, giving back to the community is another great way to celebrate business successes. This can be done through charitable donations or volunteer work, which can help to build goodwill and promote a positive company culture.

Another critical aspect of tracking your ecommerce journey is to learn from your failures. Setbacks and challenges are inevitable in any business venture. When faced with obstacles, take the time to analyze what went wrong and identify the lessons learned. Use these lessons to make better-informed decisions and continuously improve your business. One business that learned from its failures and turned around is Starbucks. In the late 2000s, Starbucks faced declining sales and a tarnished brand image due to overexpansion, high prices, and inconsistency in its products and services. This led to more than 600 stores closing and a significant decrease in profitability.

To turn things around, Starbucks embarked on a multi-year transformation plan focused on redefining the customer experience, improving product quality and innovation, and streamlining operations. The company closed underperforming stores and refocused on its core offerings, such as coffee and tea. Starbucks also invested in new technology to improve the speed and efficiency of its services, such as mobile ordering and payment.

Additionally, Starbucks revamped its brand image by emphasizing its commitment to ethical sourcing, environmental sustainability, and social responsibility. The company launched initiatives such as the "C.A.F.E. Practices" program, which ensures that its coffee is ethically sourced, and the "Grounds for your Garden" program, which repurposes used coffee grounds for gardening. These efforts helped improve Starbucks's public perception and attract new customers.

The turnaround strategy paid off for Starbucks, as the company has since experienced a resurgence in sales and profitability. Today, Starbucks operates over 31,000 stores worldwide, becoming a global symbol of premium coffee and customer experience. The company's success is a testament to its ability to learn from its failures and take decisive action to turn things around.

It's also essential to maintain a growth mindset and embrace change. The ecommerce landscape constantly evolves, with new trends, technologies, and customer preferences emerging. Stay updated with industry news, attend conferences, and network with fellow ecommerce professionals to gain fresh insights and ideas for your business. A real business that has a growth mindset is Tesla.

Despite starting as a niche electric car company, Tesla has grown into a major automotive industry player and expanded into other areas such as energy storage and solar power. This growth mindset is reflected in the company's philosophy of disruptive innovation, which has allowed it to challenge established players in the industry.

Tesla's approach to growth involves a focus on innovation, efficiency, and sustainability. The company invests heavily in research and development to create new and improved products, such as its recent launch of the Model Y electric SUV. Tesla also focuses on improving its operations and processes to increase efficiency, such as its development of the Gigafactory for battery production. Additionally, Tesla's focus on sustainability is reflected in its commitment to reducing carbon emissions, with initiatives such as its development of solar-powered charging stations and its production of energy storage systems for homes and businesses.

Furthermore, Tesla's growth mindset is reflected in its willingness to take risks and challenge established norms in the industry. The company has disrupted traditional sales models by selling directly to consumers and offering over-the-air software updates to improve its vehicles. Tesla has also taken risks in its production and delivery processes, such as its ambitious goal to produce 500,000 vehicles by the end of 2020, which it achieved despite the challenges posed by the COVID-19 pandemic.

Maintaining Work-Life Balance and Avoiding Burnout

Running an ecommerce business can be demanding, and it's crucial to prioritize your mental and physical well-being. Make time for hobbies, exercise, and socializing with friends and family. Taking care of yourself will enable you to bring your best self to your business and stay positive throughout your ecommerce journey.

Admittedly, I am not the best person to advise on work-life balance, but I assure you that setting proper habits now will help you in the future. I know all too well that finding a healthy work-life balance can feel like a daunting challenge. As an ecommerce entrepreneur, you're likely juggling multiple responsibilities and striving to grow your business. However, it's essential to prioritize your well-being and strike a balance between your professional and personal life to avoid burnout and enjoy sustainable success.

A recent study revealed that 53% of entrepreneurs experience burnout, which can lead to physical and mental health issues. Burnout symptoms include fatigue, irritability, and reduced productivity, which can harm your business in the long run. To avoid burnout, setting boundaries and managing your time effectively is crucial. Sheryl Sandberg, the COO of Facebook, emphasized the importance of work-life balance, stating that a balance between the two is necessary for happiness and productivity.

One way to maintain a healthy work-life balance is by setting realistic expectations and goals for your business. Break down your objectives into smaller, manageable tasks, and allocate specific time for each.

Allocate dedicated time for personal activities and self-care, such as exercise, hobbies, and spending time with family and friends. According to a study conducted by Harvard Business Review, regular exercise can improve mental health and increase productivity.

Another essential factor in achieving work-life balance is learning to delegate tasks and trust your team. As your ecommerce business grows, it's impossible to manage every aspect of the operation single-handedly. Delegating tasks to skilled team members can free up time for strategic decision-making and provide opportunities for professional growth. Elon Musk, the founder of Tesla and SpaceX, attributes much of his success to his ability to delegate and empower his team members.

Taking breaks and practicing mindfulness can also help you maintain a healthy work-life balance. Regular breaks can improve focus, creativity, and decision-making. Mindfulness practices like meditation or deep breathing exercises can reduce stress and improve mental well-being. Oprah Winfrey, the media mogul and philanthropist advocates for the importance of self-care and mental well-being, emphasizing that success doesn't have to come at the expense of personal happiness.

Maintaining a clear line between work and personal life is vital, especially when working from home. Designate a specific area for work and establish clear boundaries between your professional and personal life. Disconnect from work-related technology when not working to avoid constant distractions and maintain a healthy balance.

Bill Gates, a co-founder of Microsoft is known for his busy schedule, but he prioritizes time with his family and takes regular breaks from work to recharge. Gates also values philanthropy and has prioritized giving back through his foundation, which focuses on global health and education initiatives.

Arianna Huffington, the founder of The Huffington Post and CEO of Thrive Global has written extensively on the importance of prioritizing sleep and self-care. Huffington prioritizes getting a full night's sleep and avoiding technology before bed and has also incorporated practices like meditation and mindfulness into her daily routine.

Mark Zuckerberg, founder and CEO of Facebook has a busy schedule, but he prioritizes his health and well-being by exercising regularly and maintaining a healthy diet. Zuckerberg also values spending time with his family and has taken extended paternity leaves to bond with his children.

To ensure long-term success and personal well-being, finding a work-life balance is essential for ecommerce entrepreneurs. Remember, as the saying goes, "All work and no play makes Jack a dull boy." So, make time for relaxation and self-care to remain energized and focused on your journey to ecommerce success.

CHAPTER 9
BUILDING AND LAUNCHING AN ECOMMERCE WEBSITE FOR THE DO-IT-YOURSELFERS

Now that you've read the previous chapters, you should have a strong foundation for running a successful online business. You should also know about the different integrations needed, such as payment processing and shipping. Additionally, you should understand the different methods to drive your website traffic. With all that under your belt, if you decide to tackle the initial development of your website on your own, this chapter outlines a roadmap for success that can be applied to many different platforms.

Your domain name is the unique web address that represents your online store. Choose a domain name that reflects your brand and is easy to remember. Once you've chosen your domain name, select a reliable hosting provider. Many ecommerce solutions mentioned earlier in the book provide their own hosting as part of their fee structure. However, you will need hosting if you use a platform like WooCommerce or PrestaShop. In particular, I prefer hosting WooCommerce sites with companies like FlyWheel and WP Engine. They cost more than the average rates you will see advertised, but their product is far superior.

When designing a website as a non-web developer, it's essential to begin with a clear goal in mind. Determine the primary purpose of your website and the actions you want your visitors to take. This will help prioritize elements and features during the design process. To visualize the layout and structure of your site, sketch out your ideas or create a wireframe using tools like Balsamiq or Adobe XD. Balsamiq offers a 30-day free trial, with pricing starting at $9 per month after that. On the other hand, Adobe XD provides a free plan with limited features, and the premium plan starts at $9.99 per month, which includes additional features like unlimited sharing and collaboration.

In addition to wireframing tools, you can browse sites like Envato Market and ThemeForest for a wide range of premium, pre-made themes with prices ranging from $30 to $100 or more. These themes can save time and provide a professional, mobile-responsive design that can be easily customized to suit your brand and desired aesthetic.

Selecting a mobile-responsive template or theme that aligns with your brand and desired aesthetic is crucial. Platforms like WordPress, Wix, and Squarespace offer a variety of customizable templates. Keep user experience at the forefront of your design, ensure the navigation menu is simple and consistent across all pages, and use clear headings and subheadings to make content more digestible. Don't underestimate the power of whitespace; effectively using empty space around elements can create a clean, uncluttered look that enhances readability and user experience.

Maintain a consistent color scheme and typography to create a cohesive look. Prioritize loading speed by optimizing images and other elements, as a slow-loading site can frustrate users and negatively impact search engine ranking. Additionally, make sure your site is mobile-friendly, as many users access websites on smartphones or tablets. Test your site on multiple devices to ensure easy navigation and use on different screen sizes.

Invest in high-quality images, illustrations, and other visual elements that complement your content and reflect your brand identity. Make sure you have the right to use the images by licensing them from reputable sources like Getty Images, Envato Elements, or other stock photography websites. Good product photos are crucial for online sales, as studies show that 75% of online shoppers rely on product images to make a purchase decision.

Product photos play a vital role in the success of an ecommerce business, as they can significantly impact a customer's perception of the product and influence their buying decision. To create product photos that effectively sell your products, focusing on high-quality images is essential. Ensuring your product photos are crisp, clear, and high-resolution is crucial, as blurry or low-quality images can make your products appear unprofessional and unappealing. Investing in a good camera or hiring a professional photographer to capture high-quality images can make a significant difference.

Providing multiple images that showcase your product from various angles gives customers a comprehensive understanding of the item. This approach helps them visualize the product better and increases their confidence in making a purchase. Additionally, including images that demonstrate the product in use, or lifestyle images, can create an emotional connection between the customer and the product, which can lead to increased sales.

Using proper lighting is another crucial aspect of creating effective product photos. Good lighting helps accentuate the product's details, highlights its best features, and creates a professional appearance. Experiment with natural and artificial lighting to find the best option for your products.

Setting Up Your Online Store

Now that you have a plan and a design concept (or theme), it's time to set up your online store. To help, I will provide a basic guide on setting up WooCommerce, PrestaShop, Magento, Wix, Squarespace, Square Online, and BigCommerce. There are a lot of resources online to help with this including courses and YouTube videos. Many YouTube Channels also provide detailed walk-through videos to help supplement my outline.

WooCommerce Setup Outline

Set up a WordPress website by purchasing a domain from a domain registrar like Namecheap and hosting from a provider like FlyWheel or WP Engine. Install WordPress on your hosting account.

Install and activate the WooCommerce plugin from the WordPress dashboard by navigating to 'Plugins' > 'Add New', searching for WooCommerce, and clicking 'Install Now'.

Complete the WooCommerce setup wizard to configure your store's details, currency, payment gateways (such as PayPal, Stripe, or Square), and shipping options (including flat rate, free shipping, or live rates).

Choose a theme for your store by browsing the WordPress theme repository or purchasing a premium theme from a marketplace like ThemeForest. If you have a design you want to build, consider using a theme builder like Divi or Elementor.

Customize the theme's appearance and settings using the WordPress Customizer, tailoring it to your brand and products. This includes setting up your site's header, footer, homepage, and navigation menu.

Add products to your store by navigating to 'Products' in the WordPress dashboard and clicking 'Add New'. Be sure to provide essential information like the product title, description, images, price, and shipping details.

Install and configure any additional plugins for payment gateways, shipping, and other features as needed. Popular WooCommerce plugins include Yoast SEO for search engine optimization, WP Rocket for site speed optimization, and MailChimp for email marketing.

PrestaShop Setup Outline

PrestaShop requires a bit more technical knowledge to setup. You will likely need a bit more support to handle the initial steps to get the platform up and running. To begin, download the PrestaShop software from the official website (prestashop.com).

Purchase a domain and hosting compatible with PrestaShop's requirements, such as SiteGround or A2 Hosting. Upload the PrestaShop files to your server using an FTP client like FileZilla, and create a database for your store through your hosting control panel. Note, this can vary greatly across different hosting providers, but most will provide documentation or support.

Complete the installation process by navigating to your domain in a web browser and following the on-screen instructions. The PrestaShop installer will guide you through configuring your store's details, currency, and languages.

Select a theme from the PrestaShop marketplace or other third-party sources like TemplateMonster. PrestaShop themes typically have extensive documentation and support to help you customize and configure the design.

Customize your theme's appearance and configure your store settings, such as payment gateways (PayPal, Stripe, or Authorize.Net) and shipping options (local or international carriers, flat or weight-based rates).

Add products to your store through the PrestaShop dashboard by navigating to 'Catalog' > 'Products' and click 'Add New Product'. Provide essential product information, including the title, description, images, price, and shipping details.

Install additional modules for added functionality as needed. PrestaShop offers a wide range of modules in its marketplace, including options for SEO, site speed optimization, and email marketing.

Magento Setup Outline

I didn't mention it much in this book because it tends more towards larger ecommerce businesses, but Magento is a powerful platform.

Download Magento from the official website (magento.com) and choose the appropriate version for your needs, such as Magento Open Source or Magento Commerce.

Purchase a domain and hosting that meets Magento's system requirements, such as those offered by Nexcess or Cloudways. Upload the Magento files to your server using an FTP client, and create a database for your store through your hosting control panel.

Follow the Magento installation process by navigating to your domain in a web browser and completing the setup wizard. Configure your store settings, including currency, languages, and store views.

Choose a theme from the Magento marketplace or other third-party sources like TemplateMonster or ThemeForest. Magento themes often come with detailed documentation and support to help you customize and configure the design.

Customize your theme using the Magento admin panel, and set up payment gateways (such as PayPal or Amazon Pay) and shipping options (like flat rate, table rate, or carrier-based rates).

Add products to your store through the Magento dashboard by navigating to 'Catalog' > 'Products' and clicking 'Add Product'. Provide essential product information, such as the title, description, images, price, and shipping details.

Install additional extensions for added functionality as needed. Magento offers a wide range of extensions in its marketplace, including options for SEO, site speed optimization, and email marketing.

Wix Setup Outline

Creating an ecommerce website on Wix is simple:

Sign up for a Wix account and select the ecommerce plan that suits your needs, such as the Business Basic, Business Unlimited, or Business VIP plan.

Choose a template from the extensive library of ecommerce-specific designs. Wix offers a variety of templates for different industries and styles, making it easy to find one that fits your brand.

Customize your template using the Wix Editor, modifying the design, layout, and features to fit your brand. Drag and drop elements, change colors and fonts, and add pages as needed.

Configure your store settings, such as payment gateways (Wix supports popular options like PayPal, Stripe, and Square), shipping options (including flat rate, free shipping, or carrier-calculated rates), and tax settings.

Add products to your store using the Wix dashboard by navigating to 'Store Products' > 'Add New Product'. Provide essential product information, such as the title, description, images, price, and shipping details.

Publish your website and start selling. Wix handles hosting and security, so you can focus on managing your online store.

Squarespace Setup Outline

Squarespace is another all-in-one website builder with a focus on sleek, modern design. To create a Squarespace ecommerce website, follow these steps:

Sign up for a Squarespace account and choose the ecommerce plan that fits your needs, such as the Basic Commerce or Advanced Commerce plan.

Select a template from the range of ecommerce-specific designs. Squarespace templates are known for their clean, minimalist aesthetic, which can help your products stand out.

Customize your template using the Squarespace editor, adjusting the design, layout, and features to match your brand. Use the built-in style editor to change colors, fonts, and other design elements.

Set up your store settings, including payment gateways (Squarespace supports Stripe, PayPal, and Apple Pay), shipping options (like flat rate, weight-based, or carrier-calculated rates), and tax settings.

Add products to your store by navigating to the 'Pages' section in the Squarespace dashboard and clicking 'Add Product'. Provide essential product information, such as the title, description, images, price, and shipping details.

Publish your website and start selling. Squarespace takes care of hosting, security, and SSL certification, so you can focus on growing your business.

Square Online Setup Outline

Square Online is an ecommerce platform developed by the popular payment processing company, Square. It offers seamless integration with Square POS and is easy to set up. To create a Square Online store, follow these steps:

Sign up for a Square account and choose the ecommerce plan that suits your needs, such as the Free, Professional, Performance, or Premium plan.

Select a website theme from the available options, designed with various industries and styles in mind.

Customize your theme using the Square Online site editor, adjusting the design, layout, and features to fit your brand. Drag and drop elements, change colors and fonts, and add sections as needed.

Configure your store settings, such as payment gateways (Square Online supports Square payments), shipping options (including flat rate, weight-based, or carrier-calculated rates), and tax settings.

Add products to your store by navigating to the 'Items' tab in the Square dashboard, and clicking 'Add Item'. Provide essential product information, such as the title, description, images, price, and shipping details.

Publish your website and start selling. Square Online takes care of hosting and security, allowing you to focus on managing your online store.

BigCommerce Setup Outline

BigCommerce is a feature-rich, hosted ecommerce platform designed for businesses of all sizes. To create a BigCommerce website, follow these steps:

Sign up for a BigCommerce account and choose the ecommerce plan that fits your needs, such as the Standard, Plus, or Pro plan.

Select a theme from the BigCommerce theme marketplace, which offers both free and premium themes tailored to various industries and styles.

Customize your theme using the BigCommerce theme editor, modifying the design, layout, and features to fit your brand. Use the built-in style editor to change colors, fonts, and other design elements.

Set up your store settings, including payment gateways (BigCommerce supports popular options like PayPal, Stripe, and Square), shipping options (such as flat rate, weight-based, or carrier-calculated rates), and tax settings.

Add products to your store by navigating to the 'Products' section in the BigCommerce dashboard, and clicking 'Add Product'. Provide essential product information, such as the title, description, images, price, and shipping details.

Publish your website and start selling. BigCommerce handles hosting, security, and SSL certification, so you can focus on growing your business.

Customizing and Optimizing Your Website

To make your ecommerce website stand out and function smoothly, customize and optimize it using plugins and extensions. Enhance your website's functionality with features like social media integration, live chat, and more. Improve your website's performance and speed by optimizing images and caching content. Ensure that your website is mobile-friendly, as a large portion of online shopping is done on mobile devices.

SEO is crucial for improving your website's visibility on search engines and attracting organic traffic. Understand the basics of SEO and implement on-page optimization techniques, such as creating high-quality content and optimizing meta tags. Improve your website's structure and performance through technical SEO. Build quality backlinks to your website to enhance its authority and credibility through off-page SEO.

When using these platforms, follow SEO best practices to improve your website's visibility in search engines rankings. Here are some base line tips to optimize your SEO on these platforms:

Customize page titles and meta descriptions: Ensure each page on your website has a unique, keyword-rich title and a compelling meta description. These elements help search engines understand your content and display it in search results.

Crafting compelling titles and meta descriptions is an essential aspect of on-page SEO, as they influence both click-through rates and search engine rankings. To create a captivating title, keep it within 50-60 characters, ensuring that it accurately reflects the content of the page while incorporating relevant keywords. The title should be engaging and unique, piquing the user's interest and encouraging them to click through to your site. Avoid keyword stuffing or using excessive punctuation, as this can appear spammy and detract from the user experience.

Meta descriptions provide a brief summary of the content on a page and should be kept within 150-160 characters to ensure they are fully displayed on search engine results pages (SERPs). Like the title, the meta description should be engaging, informative, and include relevant keywords without appearing unnatural. A well-written meta description can significantly impact click-through rates, so take the time to craft a compelling summary that entices users to visit your site.

Optimize URLs: Use descriptive, keyword-rich URLs for your pages, as they can help improve your website's search engine rankings. Make sure to enable clean URLs in your platform's settings.

Optimizing URLs for SEO is crucial to improving search engine rankings and enhancing user experience. To create SEO-friendly URLs, it's essential to include relevant keywords that accurately describe the page's content. This helps search engines understand the page's context, and users can easily identify the content they are looking for. Keep URLs concise and straightforward, avoiding unnecessary characters, numbers, or punctuation marks that can confuse users and search engines.

Additionally, using hyphens instead of underscores to separate words in URLs is important, as search engines interpret hyphens as spaces between words. Avoid using uppercase letters; URLs are case-sensitive, and inconsistencies may lead to duplicate content issues. Lastly, maintain a consistent URL structure throughout your website, as this will help search engines to understand your site's content, ultimately improving your overall SEO performance.

Use header tags: Organize your content using proper header tags (H1, H2, H3, etc.), as search engines use them to understand the structure and hierarchy of your content.

Heading tags, ranging from H1 to H6, are used to define the structure of your content and indicate its hierarchy to both users and search engines. The H1 tag should be used for the page's main title, clearly summarizing the content and incorporating relevant keywords. There should only be one H1 tag per page to avoid confusion for search engines. H2 to H6 tags create subheadings within the content, breaking down the information into easily digestible sections.

Using heading tags improves the readability of your content for users and helps search engines understand the context and importance of different sections. It's essential to use heading tags in a logical, hierarchical order (e.g., H2 tags should be used for main subheadings, followed by H3 tags for further subsections). Including relevant keywords in your heading tags can also improve your SEO, but avoid keyword stuffing and focus on providing a clear, concise structure for your content that benefits both users and search engines.

Optimize images: Optimizing images is crucial for both SEO and user experience, as it directly affects page load times and overall website performance. To optimize images, start by choosing the right file format - typically JPEG for photos and PNG for graphics with transparency. Compressing images can significantly reduce their file size without compromising quality, leading to faster page load times. Numerous online tools and plugins are available to compress images, such as TinyPNG or ImageOptim.

In addition to compression, including descriptive file names and alt attributes for your images is essential. File names should accurately describe the image content and, where appropriate, include relevant keywords. Alt attributes provide a text alternative for users with visual impairments and search engines, offering context for the image and improving accessibility. Incorporating keywords into the alt text can further boost your SEO, but always prioritize providing a clear, accurate image description over keyword stuffing.

Add structured data: Implement schema markup to provide search engines with additional information about your content, which can lead to rich snippets and improved click-through rates.

One popular form of structured data is Schema.org markup, a collaborative effort by major search engines like Google, Bing, and Yahoo. Using Schema.org vocabulary, you can add structured data to your webpages, enabling search engines to display rich snippets, and enhanced search results that provide more information than standard search listings. Rich snippets can include ratings, prices, images, and other relevant details, making your search result more attractive and informative to users.

Implementing structured data can improve your website's search engine rankings and click-through rates, as users are more likely to click on a result that provides them with more information at a glance.

Create a sitemap and track analytics: Generate an XML sitemap to help search engines crawl and index your website more efficiently. Most platforms like Wix, Squarespace, and Square Online automatically generate a sitemap for you. WooCommerce has a variety of plugins like Yoast that will automatically handle sitemap generation as well.

Google Search Console and Google Analytics are essential tools for understanding your website's performance and user behavior. To get started, create accounts for both services, verify your website in Google Search Console, and link it to your Google Analytics account. Familiarize yourself with the dashboards, focusing on key sections like Performance and Coverage in Search Console, and Audience, Acquisition, and Behavior in Analytics.

Monitor your site's search performance, fix errors, and submit sitemaps in Google Search Console to improve search visibility. In Google Analytics, analyze traffic sources, user behavior, and set specific goals to track progress. By effectively leveraging these tools, you can make informed decisions to optimize your website and enhance user experience, boosting your online presence and conversions.

Focus on high-quality content: Publish valuable, engaging, and keyword-rich content that appeals to your target audience and helps search engines understand your website's relevance.

Google considers high-quality content informative, well-written, and engaging for users. It should provide unique insights or information not readily available elsewhere and be presented clearly and easily understandable. High-quality content should also be free of spelling and grammatical errors, demonstrate expertise in the subject matter, and be relevant to the target audience's needs. Incorporating visual elements such as images, videos, and infographics can also enhance the quality of the content, making it more engaging and shareable.

In addition to being well-crafted and engaging, high-quality content should be optimized for search engines. This means using relevant keywords strategically throughout the content without overstuffing or compromising readability.

Build quality backlinks: Encourage other reputable websites to link to your site, as backlinks are essential to search engine rankings. Engage in outreach, guest posting, and content promotion to build a strong backlink profile.

Remember that SEO is an ongoing process, and it may take some time to see the results of your efforts. Stay patient and consistently follow these best practices to improve your website's search engine performance.

Launching Your Website

Launching a new website is an exciting milestone, but the real challenge begins when it's time to announce the launch and generate initial buzz. The key to gaining traction lies in a well-planned promotional strategy that leverages various channels to attract and engage your target audience.

Your launch announcement should be attention-grabbing and provide a clear message about what your website offers. Begin by crafting an engaging and informative press release highlighting your new site's unique features, benefits, and value proposition. Use storytelling techniques to convey your brand's mission, values, and the problems your website aims to solve. Share this press release with relevant media outlets, influencers, and industry professionals to increase visibility and attract interested visitors.

Social media platforms are crucial in generating buzz for your website launch. Create captivating social media posts that tease your audience about the upcoming launch, showcasing sneak peeks of your website's features, content, or products. On launch day, share the news with a captivating post or video, and encourage your followers to visit and share the website with their networks. Be sure to engage with your audience by responding to comments, answering questions, and thanking them for their support.

Announcing your website launch and generating initial buzz requires careful planning and strategic execution. By leveraging multiple channels, such as social media, email marketing, press releases, and influencer partnerships, you can create excitement around your new site and attract genuinely interested visitors. Remember, a successful launch is just the beginning; continue to engage with your audience and refine your promotional strategies to keep the momentum going and grow your online presence.

What do I do now?

Once your website is live, it's essential to shift your focus to maintaining your site and implementing strategies to ensure the ongoing success of your e-commerce business. A well-maintained website, combined with effective business practices, can lead to increased conversions, customer satisfaction, and long-term growth.

Performing regular website maintenance is crucial for ensuring that your site remains up-to-date, secure, and functional. Routinely check for and fix broken links, update plugins and software, and ensure that your site is mobile-responsive and compatible with various browsers. Keep an eye on your site's performance metrics, such as page load time and bounce rate, and optimize accordingly to improve user experience and search engine rankings.

To keep your customers engaged and encourage repeat visits, it's essential to frequently update your site's content and inventory. Regularly publish new blog posts, articles, and other content that is relevant, informative, and valuable to your target audience. Similarly, refresh your product offerings by adding new items, updating product descriptions, and showcasing seasonal or promotional items prominently on your website.

The e-commerce landscape is continually evolving, and it's crucial to stay informed about industry trends, best practices, and emerging technologies. Invest time in learning about new marketing strategies, website optimization techniques, and customer preferences to ensure that your e-commerce business remains competitive and continues to grow. Embrace change and be open to trying new approaches to continually refine your website and business operations.

THANK YOU AND GOOD LUCK ON YOUR JOURNEY

I want to express my sincerest gratitude to each and every one of you who purchased my book. It means the world to me that you have invested your time and resources into this endeavor, and I hope that you have found value in the information provided within its pages.

My aim in writing this book was to provide a good level of baseline information and inspiration for those looking to start their own ecommerce website, whether you are taking on the challenge alone or working with a professional website developer. I believe that with the right knowledge and resources, anyone can achieve their dreams of building a successful online business.

I sincerely hope this book has given you the tools and confidence necessary to move forward in your venture. Starting an ecommerce website can be daunting, but with the right mindset and a solid foundation of knowledge, you will achieve great success.

ABOUT THE AUTHOR

Nathan Neil is a highly accomplished professional with a diverse Information System Management background. He holds a Shippensburg University Master of Business Administration and is a certified Project Management Professional (PMP). Nathan is the founder and owner of LaunchUX, a national website development agency known for delivering exceptional client results.

Nathan is an inventor with two issued US patents related to data communication across the web. He has managed multi-million-dollar projects in process improvement, manufacturing, quality control, and online sales. Nathan's expertise and contributions to the industry have been recognized by several industry publications and peer-reviewed journals where he has been published for his research work.